PRAISE FOR
SWEETIE SQUEEZE YOUR CHEEKS AND JENNIFER TIRAS

"Jennifer is a bold communicator and taught me how to have frank, tough conversations with my boys. She helps take taboo topics, remove emotion, and speak 'boy mom' in a way that penetrates their thick heads."

—LEEANN MOORE

"Raising my kids alongside Jennifer for the last twenty years has been a total blessing. She is an honest and straightforward friend—one who could always look at the little bumps in the parenting road and offer some humor, love, and advice for any situation. Love that she is sharing this with the world!"

—LISA WATSON

"I met Jenn Tiras nineteen years ago in a playgroup as a newbie mom of one; she was a seasoned mom of three. We became fast friends as I loved her candor in all things boys! Her stories were not only helpful and practical, but straight-up hysterical. To this day we reminisce all things parenting—parenthood is forever hood. I can always count on her for a good story or a nugget of good advice. You will too!"

—KATE SCHEINMAN

"Even though Jenn is younger than me, I have always looked to her for advice. Jenn is a no-nonsense mom who is not afraid to say 'no' to her kids. She knows how to get the 'job' done and has mastered the role of guiding her boys to be successful members of society while giving them enough freedom to be independent. I feel fortunate to have her in my life and thankful to share the journey of motherhood with her."

—MICHELLE BLUM

"I was blessed to meet Jenn almost twenty-five years ago (with our oldest sons) in playgroup. She has since raised four amazing boys who are now wonderful young men. I have always appreciated her parenting with logical consequences, strength, and love."

—TIFFANY LEYENDECKER

"Jenn is straightforward, loving, and full of invaluable advice and wisdom. 'Busy boys don't have a lot of time for trouble,' she would say. Her boys were active with school and sports, numerous clubs, and activities inside and outside of school. There was not a lot of downtime for anyone. Most importantly, Jenn always positioned herself to be a parent first and not a friend. Always loving and supportive, she made sure to enforce the rules made—and because consequences were carried out, not many rules were broken more than once."

—ALYSSA TIRAS

"While raising our children together, I didn't know that Jenn kept a journal of her four boys and their development from birth through leaving the nest. She doesn't claim to be a better parent or that the way she did things is the right way. What she does do is take you through her journey with an easy read that is raw and comical. Her insight, parenting tips, concern and love will keep you turning the pages."

— ELIZABETH KARKOWSKY

SWEETIE SQUEEZE YOUR CHEEKS

SWEETIE SQUEEZE YOUR CHEEKS

YOU DON'T KNOW HOW TO BE A MOM

(AND THAT'S OK—NEITHER DID I)

Advantage | Books

Published by Advantage Books, Charleston, South Carolina.
An imprint of Advantage Media.

ADVANTAGE is a registered trademark, and the Advantage colophon is a trademark of Advantage Media Group, Inc.

Printed in the United States of America.

10 9 8 7 6 5 4 3 2 1

ISBN: 978-1-64225-661-1 (Paperback)
ISBN: 978-1-64225-660-4 (eBook)

LCCN: 2023905068

Cover design by Matthew Morse.
Layout design by Matthew Morse.

This publication is designed to provide accurate and authoritative information in regard to the subject matter covered. It is sold with the understanding that the publisher is not engaged in rendering legal, accounting, or other professional services. If legal advice or other expert assistance is required, the services of a competent professional person should be sought.

Advantage Books is an imprint of Advantage Media Group. Advantage Media helps busy entrepreneurs, CEOs, and leaders write and publish a book to grow their business and become the authority in their field. Advantage authors comprise an exclusive community of industry professionals, idea-makers, and thought leaders. For more information go to **advantagemedia.com**.

To my mother: You are such a huge part of this book. Your guidance through life taught me the importance of following through and holding on to consequences. Because of your invaluable wisdom, work ethic, always putting others first, and steering me in the right direction, the content of this writing came easily. I am all of you and wouldn't be the mother I am today without your tough love. Thank you for all that you do for me and our family. I love you.

I also dedicate this book to our boys as well as the present and future children of our children. You are the reason I was inspired to write all the memories that Dad and I experienced with you.

We love you, Avery, Ryan, Reece, and Dawson.

ACKNOWLEDGMENTS

Writing this book was a lot of fun and truly helped me explore my parenting at its most intimate level. First I would like to express my thanks to Scott (the love of my life), who has been the driving force behind this book and the person who convinced me to write it, always my cheerleader—pushing me to go for it. I have also been fortunate to have some special women in my life through this entire "mommy journey." They have encouraged and supported me, but most of all been there for the ride. Love y'all!

Michelle Blum, Penny Grams, Elizabeth Karkowsky, Tiffany Leyendecker, LeeAnn Moore, Kate Scheinman, and Lisa Watson.

And to Jacqueline Guttman Dolezal, my childhood friend, who I am forever grateful to for introducing me to Scott and making all of this happen.

CONTENTS

INTRODUCTION

Fellow moms, welcome to my toolbox of tips for motherhood. Sometimes, as parents, we just accept that stressful rebellions are part of raising kids. I'm here to tell you it doesn't have to be that way!

I'm the oldest of three children, with two younger brothers, Andre and Alan. My teenage years—literally, all the way from thirteen to eighteen—probably were the worst years in my mother's life. To this very day, especially on Mother's Day, I tell her how sorry I am for the hell I put her through. She always waves it away with a proud smile, but I must have made her cry herself to sleep most nights.

The thing is we lived in the thriving, modern city of Houston, Texas, and my parents, being from Chile, had a very old-world Chilean mindset. To them life was all about family, and family certainly took precedence over friends. By my early teens, however, I knew better. Friends, of course, meant **everything**. So the clash began and continued for more than five years. I chose friends with the wildest of lifestyles, called my mother names, told her I hated her, slammed doors, broke telephones, and generally made life a living hell for the whole household.

Jenn and Mom fighting.

One incident I'd like to forget but stands out in my mind, none-theless, is a scene in the car as we were driving in our neighborhood. Inside the vehicle, my mother and I were having an all-out battle of wills. The "I hate you" mantra was flying liberally, and I actually opened the car door, while my mother was driving thirty miles per hour down our street, and just rolled out of the car. After she realized I wasn't dead, she wanted to kill me, then settled on grounding me instead. In fact I was always grounded, and it was an exceedingly difficult time of life.

If you're dealing with such a teenager right now, I can tell you that my mother's approach of "I'm not giving up on this child" formed a foundation in my life. She was as steady as a rock in her stance: I was going to follow her rules, and if I didn't, there would be consequences.

When I got to college, what do you suppose I did with all the newfound freedom? Got even wilder? Partied even harder? None of that. When I was on my own, my mother's voice was still there, and even when I hated it, it was leading me onto the right path. When I could have gotten involved with sororities and heavy partying, I didn't walk that road; instead I got married and settled down at twenty-one, earned my degree, and today I give all the credit to her for influencing me. She made photo albums, and so do I—along with journaling and scrapbooking; she was a teacher, and I became a teacher; she was highly organized, and I added organizational systems to motherhood; she was consistent in her parenting, and I've learned that consistency is the most effective parenting tool there is.

From my experiences as the one being heavily disciplined and the one doing the disciplining, along with my early childhood development training, I have created some tips to help avoid behavior issues. I'll be honest: the influence my mom and my husband had over me in developing these tips cannot be overstated. Here are six themes you'll see repeated in different ways throughout the book:

> **My mother's approach of "I'm not giving up on this child" formed a foundation in my life.**

Be Consistent and Follow Through: I was nineteen when I met Scott, still living at home, and we knew instantly that we were in love. Now, he was almost ten years older than I was, so my mom was on *high* alert when we first got together.

I'd be getting ready for a date, and there she'd be, fishing for details. I'm not talking about simple-curiosity questions like, "Oh, where are you going?" No, it was an interrogation. She needed to know the name of the restaurant, the title of the movie we were going to see, which theater it was playing at, on and on ... this was a *major* inconvenience, because I *wasn't* actually at the movie. Now I had to get details from friends who had seen it—because there was no doubt my mom would be there, waiting for me when I got home, at midnight on the dot, per her rules.

Scott and Jenn dating.

I had to be on my toes, with full-on makeup, lipstick, and neat hair, like a respectable young lady should look at the end of a date. Then she would sit in the bedroom with me and *follow through*: "What did you eat at the restaurant? What was the movie about? Was it sad? Exciting? Gory? What happened in the end?" I had to really concentrate to know what I was telling her.

Of course I'm doing the same to my kids. You bet I check on them when they tell me they'll be sleeping overnight at a friend's house. Yes, I do call the mom, just like my mother used to; and yes, I drive them to the event.

Recently, Dawson, my youngest, was invited to a party, and when I pulled up to the home, there was a security guard stationed outside. My son saw the guard, guessed that this would send me flying to the door to speak with the parents, and immediately started pleading, "Mom, please don't get out of the car; it's so embarrassing; there are girls right there!"

I said, "Well, I won't get out of the car and embarrass you, but I'm just going to roll on over to the security guard and have a chat with him."

Excessively relieved, my son agreed, "Okay; that's fine, Mom. Just don't go to the door."

Meanwhile I'd gone to school with the mom of that house, and she and I had already spoken. She assured me she would be there all night, then told me they had hired the security guard—*follow through*.

Best Friends? No—Just No! A parenting style that's currently popular is one of moms and dads wanting to be best friends with their kids instead of being parents. They want to be the cool mom, the one who serves the alcohol, takes them to concerts late at night, and gets drunk and carefree with them.

My mom was *never* that mom. By the time we started driving, none of my friends in high school had curfews. They could spend the night wherever they wanted, and their moms wouldn't call and check on them.

To my utter humiliation and traumatization, my mom would call the parent or walk right up to the door and introduce herself! "Hey, Mrs. Smith, I just want to make sure you're going to be here, because my daughter says she's spending the night." No one else did this! Why was she so controlling? How could I face my friends ever again?

What were the results of this type of fight, consistency, and follow-through? Well, I was never able to get away with going to a party and spending the night somewhere when the parents were actually in Europe. I also wasn't there when a few kids became too rowdy, when someone got beat up, and when the cops came and broke the party up.

Although *I did almost die* of embarrassment on several occasions, I now know, 100 percent, that my mother was right, and I proudly employ the same standards, methods, and torment.

Consistency Turns to Real Friendship: You don't have to worry that you'll *never* be friends with your child if you choose consistency and tough love. The circle of life dictates that these things will flip-flop as the child gets older. They will come to understand and even thank you for your effort.

During the most turbulent of my teenage years, when I was not listening to anything my mother said because she obviously didn't understand life, she managed to get through to me in a way that literally set me on the correct course.

All through high school, I dated a guy who was verbally and emotionally abusive. My mom, understanding that trying to force us apart would only drive me directly into his clutches, never tried to demand a breakup. *(Did I mention she must have cried herself to sleep many nights?)* Instead, seeing me in a constant state of sadness, she would try to convince me that this guy was all wrong for me. She'd say, "Look at yourself; you're crying, miserable, and depressed. Don't you think there's something better for you out there?"

Turns out, when "something better" presented itself, it was like her words conjured up a picture, and I could clearly see that everything she was saying was right. Scott walked into our lives like a breath of fresh air. All my friends were like, "How are your parents happy you're dating someone nine-and-a-half years older than you?"

Well … you're welcome to answer that for yourself. After all, this is a book on parenting. What would you do? How would you feel? Here's the story:

After high school I was gifted with a trip to Paris. The whole time I was gone, the ex-boyfriend obsessed over the separation. When I returned and got into college, he started stalking me. Things were getting very scary, and a few times I had to park my car inside my parents' garage to avoid him.

I had absolutely moved on, however, and as part of that process, I started pursuing work in an office environment. High school was over, and I was "done" working at places like Chuck E. Cheese (yep, I worked there). Working in a business office felt more like the change I needed. A friend of mine from childhood, Jacqueline, was able to get me an interview for a receptionist position in her father's office, and I got the job.

On my second day, still unsure of everything, I was sitting in my boss's office, when in walked Scott. He had a Tarzan-dark tan and was carrying an eight-inch-high stack of topless photographs from a recent trip to Greece he'd taken with his buddies. He had come in to show these photos to my boss, Diana. Well, there I was, so naturally she introduced me to him.

The sparks that flew were immediate, and I found myself blushing and nervous. From there I made sure to run into him whenever possible. Shortly afterward Jacqueline, beaming and scrambling to talk to me, revealed that Scott, having found out that we were friends, had been asking her all kinds of questions about me. I was, of course, over the moon with this news. He was *so cute!*

A few months later, there was an office pool party at a coworker's home. All of us were gathered around the pool eating, drinking, and talking. I happened to be looking across the pool and saw a toddler fall in. It was actually Jacqueline's son, Patrick. Absolutely no one noticed he was drowning. Fully dressed, I dove into the pool and pulled him up to the surface for air. Yes, my maternal instincts were strong even at age nineteen. Scott witnessed all of this happen and was locked in; he was *mine*.

Scott and Jenn's third date.

When we went on our first date, Scott picked me up at my house to meet my parents. Before the date I asked my mom to give me a quick wink letting me know if she liked Scott. So he arrived, shook hands with my dad, and politely introduced himself to my parents. I happened to glance over at my mom, and there she was, blinking like a broken turn signal with both eyes.

By our third date, we had this talk about whether or not we wanted to see anybody else. We both agreed that we wanted to be exclusive with each other. I knew I was going to marry him, and he knew he was going to marry me.

Chilean family.

Here was this older guy; he had a job; he was respectful and educated, and he was treating me like a queen. My parents adored him from the start (even my dad), and my mother just knew it was right. She was so glad I was out of that dysfunctional relationship that she welcomed Scott right away. In the process of this, we grew closer and closer, and I got a chance to see that my mom really was the rock in my life who loved me through it all.

Scott and I dated for about a year before we got engaged. He even flew to Chile and met my entire South American family. Even though Scott's Spanish was "muy malo" and they called him "gringo loco," they graciously welcomed him into the family. Soon thereafter Scott asked my dad for my hand. My parents had no problem at all with the age gap.

Scott and Jenn engaged in Portugal, 1992.

Be Sneaky, or They Will Be: Sneakiness was also a favorite tactic of my mother's, and I've taken that on as an actual parenting style. Back in the day, we didn't have texting, so friends wrote handwritten notes to each other, on notebook paper, sometimes with sparkling pastel ink. With zero respect for my personal privacy, my mom would go in my room and search, then *read my notes!* I had to start tearing them into a million pieces so she couldn't read them. It didn't matter. I discovered she was piecing them together like a puzzle. This meant war! So I took my special, saved notes and decided to burn them in the bathroom trashcan. *Yes, I almost set the house on fire!*

Of course, I do the same types of things; I just don't get caught as often, and my kids probably don't know I'm as sneaky as I am. I've learned that there are some very innovative places where a teenager can hide things. Here is a partial list of places I've found some interesting items in—parents, you'll want to brace yourself for what you might find:

- Inside socks
- Inside shoes
- Inside pockets
- Inside backpacks
- Under the mattress
- Under the bed
- Garage
- Attic
- Their phones (secret apps behind other apps)
- Their social media *(learn the different social media sites, if you have to, so you can be in the loop)*

Very simply if they know you will be checking on them, your sneakiness is the best deterrent to their own sneaky behavior.

One-on-One Time Is Crucial: When I was growing up, dads supported the family financially, and moms were home to deal with whatever was happening in the children's lives. Today, most parents, out of necessity, work full-time jobs, and it's not as easy to keep up with the day-to-day. I can't stress this enough, from a mom-and-educator point of view: make it a point to have one-on-one time with your children, whether you have one or a bunch of them. You will be glad you did it, and you will create bonding memories that the child will never forget. You are also building family traditions that, hopefully, they'll continue with their own children one day.

Put the Responsibility on _Them_: The very same day I began this book, I kid you not, I got a text from a fellow mom that said, "I love how you parent."

I was caught off guard; like, why is she randomly texting me, "I love how you parent"?

I responded, "Ha, ha, ha. Why are you saying that?"

She said, "Because you have the kids being responsible for what they should be responsible for."

To bring in a bit of context, my son, along with a few others in the same age group, were planning a trip to Israel. One of the moms asked if the boys needed to get a COVID test before leaving on that trip, and if they did, had they arranged for it?

> **You can't protect them from everything, so you must, as a good parent, teach them to handle themselves.**

These "kids" are twenty-two years old. I responded, "I'm not even asking my son about COVID testing for the trip to Israel. I'm letting him handle it and not getting involved; they're adults."

When I share things like that, along with the techniques I use to ensure responsible, well-behaved kids, not everyone texts me a warm fuzzy about my parenting style. I'm sure some people will think I'm crazy, too harsh, maybe too demanding. That's okay. Take whatever you can get from my collection of tips and stories, and adjust it to your own style. Bear in mind, as you move forward, you will not be there to protect them on the first job interview; you won't be there if kids at school cause trouble for them; you can't protect them from everything, so you must, as a good parent, teach them to handle themselves.

• • •

The success I've seen in my own home and in the lives of others is what inspires me to write this book. I've stood in line, sat around at sporting events, and talked with other moms who say, "That tip is a great idea; will you send that to me? Why didn't I think of that? I need to do that."

When Scott and I travel on his business trips, the subject of motherhood often comes up—possibly because I love to talk to people, especially moms in the early stages of motherhood. I can be pretty expressive, even raw sometimes, but we almost always get into a great conversation, even have a laugh or two over the challenges motherhood presents.

Besides my desire to talk to moms, however, I did achieve all of the educational requirements too, like graduating from the University of Houston in 1994, magna cum laude, with a degree in early childhood development. No form of education or influence from any one person, however, can prepare you for sleeplessness, messy accidents, and raging ear infections running through your home. I'm not a doctor, and any tips I present are from my own experience as a mom. If at any point you question anything during your parenting journey, whether physically, mentally, emotionally, or otherwise, be sure to contact your physician for guidance.

That said, from mom to mom, we'll discuss what to expect during pregnancy and how to survive the newborn, toddler, and elementary years. We'll also get candid and open about how to approach the middle school, high school, and young adult eras. Let's talk charts and contracts—yes, contracts—for phone and driving privileges.

I hope you laugh all the way through the book; I hope you post sticky notes all over the pages, so you can refer back to that section as you get there; most of all I hope you know you're doing a phenomenal job. If you can take a tip or two and use it for your own parenting tool bag, my goal for this book will be accomplished.

Let's start at the beginning—I mean the *very* beginning, before your baby is even conceived. I'm sure you have big plans. Let's try to put some of those plans into perspective as you dream during the prebaby season of motherhood.

CHAPTER 1

CONCEPTION AND PREBABY

Knowing you want a baby and setting out to get pregnant are, quite possibly, some of the most exciting times of life. You are probably dreaming of how it's going to be. Maybe your dream is so detailed that you feel it should play out just as you perceive it. This is what happened to me, and it's probably safe to say that not *everything* will go exactly as expected.

After Scott and I got married, the plan was to have a big family—three, maybe four kids. Of course, we were naive and young, and we felt that, surely, we would get just what we wanted, a boy and a girl—no problem! So off we went into the "trying" phase. This should only take a month, right? I mean we're both strong and robust.

I bolstered my optimism again the next month and told myself the same thing: it won't take long; by next month, for sure, we'll be pregnant.

Six months later hope had turned to dread, and dread almost turned to panic. We weren't getting pregnant. I started thinking about adoption. Scott went for testing, and it was proven that he was healthy and capable of reproducing. My God, did this mean it was all on me?

Married March 27, 1993.

A few more months went by, and in desperation, feeling like my whole life could be altered because of this, I knew I had to call Dr. Stanley Connor. He was my mother's ob-gyn; he had delivered me; and now he was my ob-gyn. I trusted him implicitly. With a sinking heart, I looked at Dr. Connor, knowing he would feel my pain, and I said, "Dr. Connor, it's the worst! I think I have fertility issues because I'm doing everything I'm supposed to do and I'm just not getting pregnant." I was in tears at this point. I was so distraught about it.

Dr. Connor did not seem as upset as I thought he should be. In fact he looked at me quite calmly and told me two things: "learn your body" and "relax."

Learn/Know Your Body: There are women who know exactly when they're ovulating, and they know that they'll start their menstrual cycle on such-and-such day every single month. For me, one month I would have a cycle and another month I wouldn't; one month I'd start on the fifteenth, and the next month it started on the eighth, a full week early. I had to learn my own body by the way I was feeling, using certain indicators to let me know where I was in my cycle.

Relax: Dr. Connor's next piece of advice is what really did the trick. This medical giant gave me this prescription: he said, "You're basically having intercourse just to get pregnant instead of enjoying the moment. Stop obsessing over getting pregnant; go get a bottle of wine, have a nice dinner, and relax and enjoy each other."

The next month, I was finally pregnant!

THE OVULATION KITS

One of the ways I learned to know my body was by using ovulation kits. These testing kits will let you know when you're ovulating so you can take action to conceive. If I could add up the amount of money we spent on these kits, I'm fairly certain we could take a lavish vacation around the globe.

We really started using ovulation kits specifically as a "tool" with our third child. Our second pregnancy happened right away and went along smoothly—except ... it was another boy. I began worrying now. Shouldn't the children arrive "boy, girl" or something like that?

We were inspired on the third one to target our efforts. Life was moving forward, the family was growing, and we wanted to build a house. My pregnancies so far, though, had been very difficult during the first four months. I was physically ill all day long. A certain smell would set me off, and I would projectile vomit until I was weak.

I felt that the only way I could face the challenge ahead was to schedule the pregnancy, and this time I had to have a girl! If this wasn't going to happen for us organically, then we were prepared to make it happen intentionally. Certain of our own control over this thing, we decided to buy the book *How to Choose the Sex of Your Baby* by Landrum B. Shettles.[1] Here is the basic premise:

DR. SHETTLES'S TIP #1

(BY RACHEL GUREVICH AT VERYWELLFAMILY.COM)

If you want to have a boy, Shettles's theory advises having sexual intercourse as close to ovulation as possible—ideally, within 12 hours before your expected ovulation.

The method also calls for avoiding sex (or using contraception) until you reach this time. The theory is that the Y-sperm cells will arrive at the egg faster, or before, the X-carrying sperm cells can.

If you want to have a girl, on the other hand, the theory holds that you should have sex every day once your period ends, up until two to four days before you expect to ovulate. Then, avoid sex. The method also calls for avoiding sex (or using contraception) when you have the most fertile cervical mucus present.

The theory is that the X-carrying sperm cells are slower swimmers but will survive longer than the Y-sperm cells, and only X-carrying sperm cells will still be there when the egg is ovulated.

---

1   Landrum B. Shettles, *How to Choose the Sex of Your Baby*, revised and updated edition (New York: Harmony, 2006).

We read this book from cover to cover, took notes, highlighted relevant sections, and started buying ovulation kits. I went on the special diet they recommend for conceiving a girl; I did handstands after sex—literally I got pinned upside down against the wall—because another theory convincingly explained that this downward trajectory would assist the sperm in finding their target.

I was certain that ovulation kits were the answer, an absolute shoo-in for a pregnancy of my timing, resulting in the baby girl I wanted so badly. It was science, right? The ovulation kit would let me know when I was ovulating; I would arrange intercourse at the correct moment; and voila, a girl should be forthcoming. What could go wrong?

We did get pregnant, just as we wanted to ... and when the baby was born, we looked into the third most beautiful face we had ever seen: Reece, our brand-new bouncing baby boy!

My tip here is really more of a realization: half the people who read that book will be satisfied customers and swear to its absolute truth. The other half of us ... not so much!

PLAN EVERYTHING ... THEN BE FLEXIBLE

With each child, of course, we were thrilled to welcome him, and we couldn't imagine life without him being exactly who he is. During the planning stages, over all of those years, however, I got really hung up with the whole obsession of having a daughter. There is just something special about a mother/daughter relationship. Even though I wouldn't trade my sons for anything, I wanted to share that same closeness with a daughter of my own. At this point in my life, my mother is my best friend, so I wanted to experience the same relationship with a daughter.

When I finally realized this dream wasn't coming true, it took me a long time to get over it. After much soul searching, I came to the conclusion that God gives us the right things for the right reasons. I look at my friends who have daughters now, and I truly don't think I would have been a good girl mom; I'm so much better, more natural and perceptive, as a boy mom.

Once I did accept my fate as an exclusively boy mom, I decided to turn it all around. If I saw my friends taking their daughters to get their nails done, why couldn't I take my sons for a pedi and a mini massage while I got my mani? It didn't make them feminine by any means. It did create a closeness and an openness that we still share today.

So, yes, definitely have a plan, and enjoy making that plan a reality. Just keep in mind that if your plan doesn't go as planned, work within yourself to accept what you have and move on, because you can dwell on it until you make yourself sick, and it's not going to change a thing.

A DOZEN TIPS TO PREPARE YOURSELF FOR MOTHERHOOD

At times most of us older moms look back and assess our progress. As they say, hindsight is twenty-twenty. If I were to go back, I think I would pay close attention to these twelve things during the conception and prebaby stage of motherhood.

Troubled Relationship? Babies Won't Help! My first tip is somewhat of a warning: if you're having trouble in your relationship with your spouse/partner and you get the idea that having a baby will solve things, think again! Flat out, all it will do is magnify the tension. Please don't bring a child into that situation. Be very sure you and your spouse/partner are healthy and ready for the stress of this commitment. (And oh boy will there ever be stress!)

Nutrition: A friend recently began talking about getting pregnant, and of course she was ecstatic about welcoming a new baby. This premom happened to be a smoker, and I was a bit concerned when she continued smoking, even after announcing that they were "trying." She had a mild medical condition that could flare during pregnancy, and smoking added serious health risks to her situation. When I gently brought this up, she replied that she planned to make health changes, including quitting smoking, the minute she got pregnant. Many premoms tackle healthcare and nutrition with this plan.

I approached prebaby nutrition in a polar-opposite way. My theory was to create the most nutrient-dense, safest-possible environment for the baby. So I started taking prenatal vitamins and lots of folic acid before we even started trying. I customarily enjoyed a glass of wine or two on a Saturday evening, and I even stopped that. I really started to cleanse my body well ahead of time.

Each mom will decide the best course of action to take for her own body. Premoms in the planning stages, think carefully about this topic, as your decision may directly affect your growing baby.

Don't Do It Alone: As women we often develop a sense of responsibility that drives us to play Superwoman: "I can do it all, all by myself!" Maybe, for private reasons of your own, you're even trying to prove that to someone.

This is a serious mistake when it comes to caring for an infant. Raising a baby is hard; having an emotionally and physically helpless little person attached to you 24-7, with no help, is likely to drive you crazy and take away from your best parenting instincts.

If people ask how they can help, tell them, especially a good friend, "I need a meal train. I need someone to watch the baby while

I take a shower and grocery shop. I need help with housekeeping, because I can't seem to keep up." Be open about it; laugh it off if you feel embarrassed; and don't try to be superhuman.

One great way to find support is through a childbirth education class, such as Lamaze. Your doctor will help steer you toward these types of classes during your sixth month or so. What you'll find in these gatherings is a ready-made group of people, all living around the same general distance from the hospital, all having babies at the same time. If you think about it, this group can be an amazing support.

Don't try to be superhuman.

We actually became close friends with several couples from our Lamaze group. We saw them every two weeks or so for the classes, and we all had our babies, of course, around the same time. From there we started playgroups, had dinner at one another's homes, and went on outings together, such as trips to the zoo—and we remain close to this very day. We helped each other, and in different ways we still do today.

Moms Who Are Working Outside the Home: A young nurse who works out of my doctor's office recently told me she was beginning to try to get pregnant. I had recurring visits to this doctor, so each time I saw him, I'd eagerly wait to see if she was pregnant yet.

During one visit she expressed her desire to stay home once she did have a baby. I asked her if she was able to do that, and she revealed something to me that I did not really have to deal with when my children were small. She said that in her field if she leaves the job for any length of time, she will lose her position, and all of her certifications may go out the window. That makes for extremely difficult decisions for professional moms.

Reece's playgroup.

Ryan's playgroup.

Young moms today have this type of pressure to contend with all of the time. At the school where I work, they are opening a room for babies ages eight weeks old through fifteen months. I was astounded by this. I remember feeling completely unable to get into the swing of life after childbirth, much less to go back to work so soon. When I questioned the administrative staff, they responded that they were doing this because there was such a high demand for childcare in this age group that they felt it necessary to expand.

Typical labor laws allow a new mom twelve weeks to recover and bond with her new baby. If you're planning to return to work, you must start thinking ahead of time about how you will handle childcare. The very luckiest among us have a parent or relative who loves the child who will step into this role. Most don't have this luxury. Many grandmothers today are still working; sometimes they live out of state, or there are health or safety issues that prevent grandparents from helping.

If this is your situation, you will have to clearly think about childcare and what kind of budget you have to make that happen. Keep in mind, your emotional attachment to the baby takes over your entire being. The decision isn't simply made with your logic and reasoning; it's made with your maternal heart, and it's nearly impossible to ignore what it tells you.

If you want to stay home with your child, there is some statistical evidence that may support this decision. Now I know every job, woman, and household is different, but the chart below can give you an idea of how the working mom's paycheck, specifically, gets affected when children come into the home.

2022 Women's Weekly Median Income (U.S. Bureau of Labor Statistics)[2]	$943/wk
Monthly Income	$3,772/mo
MONTHLY EXPENSES FOR WORKING MOMS:	
Childcare (nat'l avg. for working moms)	$1,230/mo
Gasoline (nat'l avg. is between $400-$1,301)	$600/mo
Groceries/Toiletries (makeup, lunches/eating out, etc.)	$600/mo
Additional Car Insurance (rates lower when driving less.)	$50/mo
Clothing Savings (nat'l avg. for working moms)	$200/mo
Car Loan/Expense (if you're able to reduce to one car)	$400/mo
Total Expenses	**$3,080/mo**
Monthly Income after Expenses	$692/mo
Weekly Income after Expenses	$173/wk
Taxes also decrease when income decreases, and there are tax benefits for some families when income is lowered. (Check with your tax professional for details.)	

Working from Home: There are many work-from-home opportunities for employment today, and many moms-to-be seek jobs so they can be home with their children and still bring income into the household. This is a fantastic option for many moms.

One caution to consider: it's extremely hard to concentrate when your baby has needs and you're legitimately busy working. My tip would be, if you can, to have someone help you with childcare, even though you're there. You are still able to supervise and be present, but

---

2   US Bureau of Labor Statistics, "News Release: Usual Weekly Earnings of Wage and Salary Workers Fourth Quarter 2022," July 19, 2022, https://www.bls.gov/news.release/pdf/wkyeng.pdf.

for those hectic moments, another capable and loving person is there to step in. Reliable teenagers are often eager for this type of interaction, and their pay won't break the bank.

If this isn't possible for you, you may have to do what busy moms have done for centuries: work when the baby sleeps.

Babysitting for Income: These days babysitters make between fifteen and twenty dollars an hour. If you have the temperament to care for other children in your home, you can make a good living and give another mom peace of mind in the process.

These moms will literally create a family atmosphere in their home, and they welcome other children into it. It's very important that moms who plan to take in other children for income feel this way. You would not want your child in the care of someone who is "only in it for the money," and you should not take this responsibility on if that is your focus.

All of that said, if you're one of those amazing moms who love having kids around, you're wanted and needed, and the money can be outstanding.

Quality Childcare … without Charge: As we previously mentioned, babysitters make between fifteen and twenty dollars per hour. Now if you're making that kind of money, fantastic; however, if you're the one paying it out, it can absolutely kill a budget.

Swapping childcare services with other moms is one way to find quality, caring sitters without having to pay—at least not in cash. One mom may take your children this Saturday night, but then the next time she needs a sitter, you swap services and provide quality, attentive care to her kids. This can work in many wonderful ways if you find the right parents to work with. (Again, that childbirth education class may be a helpful resource.)

Your Body Will Change: One of the most unexpected realities new moms face is the way their body changes after birth. We all know about the adorable, round belly and some necessary weight gain, but that's where the image ends. We tend not to think about how the body changes once the baby arrives. To be fair, there are those women who can deliver their baby and their belly button pops back normally, and they are able to wear their skinny jeans. I want you to know, for the rest of us, this is wrong on every level.

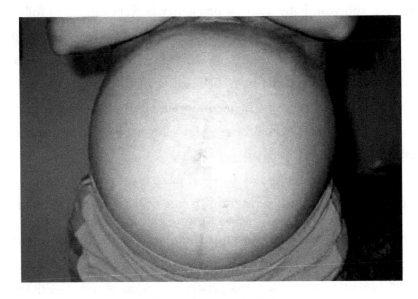

Jenn nine months pregnant with Avery.

The truth is most of us experience stretch marks, saggy skin, a distorted belly button, and weakness in the abdominal muscles. A friend of mine tells of having her first child at twenty-one years old. Lying in the hospital bed, she looked at her belly as the nurse examined her. She was confused; it looked like lines of rubber bands under her skin had appeared and then been stretched to a point of distortion. The new mom asked the nurse what the lines were. With a gentle smile, the nurse informed her that they were stretch marks.

Innocently this twenty-one-year-old looked at the nurse with a distasteful expression and asked, "When do they go away?"

The nurse chuckled and responded, "They don't."

It's a harsh reality to face when your young, firm body is suddenly sagging, and your muscles can no longer fully control your urine stream. It can be utterly depressing. That's why I feel it's important to understand this part of the motherhood package beforehand.

Begin exercising now as a way to create a healthy environment for you and your baby. During pregnancy be very careful to follow your doctor's advice regarding how strenuous exercise should be in the various phases of carrying the child. At one point I had to use a belly band to keep the baby belly from hitting my pelvic bone during routine maneuvers (so uncomfortable). After the baby arrives, continue the routine of exercising, again following your doctor's advice until you're fully recovered.

I subscribe to the theory that if it takes nine months to put the weight on, it will take nine months to take the weight off. Plan on it.

Lining Up Your Help: The first three months of mothering a newborn are filled with learning curves, adjustments, and unsettled feelings. (Did I mention a tiny, helpless person is in need of you 24-7?) You will need and appreciate all of the help you can get, and prebaby is the time to line it up.

As I mentioned, the easiest way to ask for help is to talk to some of your closest friends and family about what you need and ask them to make the requests. For instance, a meal train, light housekeeping, or "shower" sitters—those who sit with the baby while you shower—for the first four weeks after childbirth will be an inexpressible blessing. Your friends and family can help set that up for you so you don't have to ask people yourself. If this is a second or third child, maybe arrangements can be made for someone to take the older children out for a while, so you can have some time with the new baby.

When I had Dawson, my fourth son, my friend Kate would regularly take Reece for a while. She'd bring him and her son out for ice cream or arrange a playdate after school. Scott then would pick Reece up on his way home from work. These days were golden to me because I had the whole day to adjust with the new baby. In turn, when Kate needed childcare, I stepped in to assist.

Just a Minute … Please? Okay, I've reiterated this a few times now, so I'm sure you get it, but another shock to new moms is the obvious-but-commonly-overlooked reality that a living, helpless, tiny person is going to be with you all the time. For the most part, this is expected, and you have planned for everything. The simplest tasks, however, like using the restroom or taking a shower, may leave you utterly perplexed once the child is in front of you. What is to be done with the baby while I blissfully douse myself in a thunderous cascade of hot water? What if they need me? What if a sudden danger arises, and I'm not there?

This is where a shower sitter will literally change your world. If you don't have someone to sit with the baby during this time, the easiest tip in the toolbox is to put the baby in an infant sleep chair or bouncy seat; place it where you can see and hear the baby; then allow yourself the relaxation you need. Every few minutes peek out and assure yourself that the baby is safe and sound.

If your baby is having a particularly fussy day, try soothing music to calm them. If they cannot be calmed … it's okay. Most of us moms understand the need for skipping the shower altogether some days, when necessary.

Quote It! We used quotes to quickly and easily reinforce values that we wanted our sons to remember. It's amazing the number of times per day that some situation will require the perfect quote. Our full list is 162 strong, and I use them all regularly. If you'd like to see the full list, it's located in the back of the book. Otherwise, here are our top-ten favorites.

1.   Once you learn to quit, it becomes habit.
2.   Whatever you are, as you become older, you become more of it.
3.   Bite off more than you can chew—and chew like hell!
4.   No one has ever drowned in their own sweat.
5.   If you're going to be stupid, you better be tough.
6.   Sometimes what seems life changing right now really won't be that important tomorrow.
7.   Practice like someone is always watching.
8.   Be kind: everyone you meet or know is fighting their own fierce battle.
9.   When you marry the girl, you marry the whole family.
10. Don't expect anything from anyone, and you'll be pleasantly surprised.

Find Time to Record the Memories: Again, for premoms this is something to be aware of, so you can take action: the speed at which your new baby will grow will absolutely astound you. Do whatever you can to make a record of the memories. Keep your journal or electronic record handy so you can add things as they come up. Document anything you want to. If they say something silly or do something new, write it down!

Journaling became a big part of motherhood for me, but for a very practical reason: I have a terrible memory, and I know it. My cousin Vivi, understanding this challenge, gifted me a journal, and I committed myself to writing out what was happening to me as a mom and how I felt about it all. It started out simply enough … but then … those tiny babies started growing and began to do, and say, the funniest things! I was furiously writing out sentences on Post-it notes, if necessary, just to get the memory into some written form.

Jenn's journals.

Moms today might use a cell phone or computer to streamline this, but back then we didn't walk around with a video camera, and iPhones weren't invented. If I were a new mom right now, I would absolutely be doing a Shutterfly book for all of my kids. The point is to make a record of the child's life to one day pass on to them. I specifically wanted a place to write very personal things to each of my boys because I knew one day I'd be gone, and this would be something of me they would value.

When I suggest finding time to record your memories, oftentimes the response I get is that there just isn't time for the luxury of collecting memories. I get it; I don't have the time either. I find it impossible to journal every day, as my schedule is typically crazy. The way I manage it is by sticking those quickly written Post-it notes inside of my journal, and when I get some free time, I arrange them correctly. In fact I just went out of town, and I took my journal with me. Instead of watching a movie on the plane, I entered over three months' worth of Post-it memories into my journal.

Mommy journaling is, in fact, a main theme of the book, and you'll find a journaling tip at the end of each chapter. Now that my sons are older, I can tell you that making a record of their memories has become a treasure for all of us. In the beginning you're writing about all the baby milestones, and then you'll come to see that you're writing about your son's first date, college acceptance, or family vacations, etc. Plan to make it a priority from day one so time doesn't slip away from you.

> **Making a record of their memories has become a treasure for all of us.**

• • •

The conception and prebaby stage of motherhood, as you can see, is a wonderful yet serious time of dreaming and planning. You're almost there, pregnant and awaiting a beautiful phase of your life. Let's talk about expecting: the highs, the lows, and what the reality of pregnancy is all about.

• • •

JOURNALING TIPS FOR THE CONCEPTION AND PREMOM STAGE

THE GIFT OF PHOTOS!

This tip came to me by necessity, really. When our children were small, we used a camera to take pictures—a separate piece of equipment from our phones. We had to buy film, take our pictures with it, then bring the film to a developing station, usually located at drugstores throughout town. Of course, we would accidentally get duplicates or a photo would have a blurry face in the background, so we devised a way to highlight the extras.

Whenever we give cards or gifts for anniversaries, birthdays, thank you notes, or any other occasion, we add a relevant photo to the card. People love this! For instance, every time I write Scott an anniversary card, I put a picture of us in it. When we give my parents a holiday card, we might include a photo of the kids around the Christmas tree when they were small.

We also personalize gifts by putting a photo of the recipient right on the package. This works great during the holidays when many gifts and givers are flying about. The kids look for their photo, and they know that gift is for them.

Chances are young moms today have most of their photos on their phones, but if this idea appeals to you, you can do this by simply printing the relevant photo and attaching it to your gift.

CHAPTER 2

PREGNANCY

Pregnancy is unique for each and every woman, and each will have her own sets of circumstances and ways to cope. Some women experience superior health, and they are able to stay active all nine months. Some start out this way, then develop conditions that require bed rest for the last few months of pregnancy. Still others are put on bed rest for the entire duration of their pregnancy.

I want to reiterate that I'm not a medical professional, and in no way are my experiences exhaustive. You will get valid insight from many moms as you go. After all I went through to get pregnant, though, I was honed in to the experience. From a mom who's been there, here are the very first signs that I've observed when a woman is pregnant:

Sign #1 Exhaustion: Typically the first thing you may notice, before any other signs of pregnancy, is a feeling of exhaustion. This isn't an ordinary "down" day, nor can it be explained by a poor night's rest. This exhaustion goes into your bones, if possible, and it demands sleep.

If you recall in the last chapter, I encouraged moms to start a health regimen before becoming pregnant. This is one of the reasons

I suggest this. If you're strong, nourished, and in good health, you have your best chance of combating the exhaustion stage of pregnancy.

Sign #2 Low-Back Aches or Cramps: Low-back cramping is a sign that we often don't correlate to pregnancy. For some women, that low-back ache is one of the very first signs, and it often goes unnoticed or is explained away by physical exertion or the expectation of their period.

Sign #3 Oily Skin: I remember feeling like my face got oilier or greasier—it seemed like it would almost glisten. This, again, is the result of hormonal changes in the body. I felt like I had to wash my face three times a day, and my tip would be to do so, if you're able.

Sign #4 Breast Tenderness: You know the breast tenderness that comes just before your period? Pregnancy breast tenderness will feel the same way, but it doesn't go away. The beginning of your milk production has started, and this tenderness will likely be with you in varying stages throughout the pregnancy.

Sign #5 Aroma Not-Therapy: One night during my first pregnancy, Scott was trying to help by bringing dinner home. Poor Scotty didn't know what hit him. I don't think he even walked through the door, and a whiff of barbecue chicken sent me diving for the kitchen sink. To this day the memory is almost physical, and I'm not a fan of barbecue chicken.

Beware of smells, especially during the "morning" sickness phase of pregnancy.

NAUSEA, NOT NECESSARILY A MORNING THING

A large percentage of pregnant moms experience about three months of "morning sickness." This means that, working hand in hand with exhaustion, they feel sick to their stomach when they wake up, sometimes resulting in vomiting, but not always.

I know women who have zero sickness throughout their pregnancies. I also know women who have literally nine months of exhaustion, nausea, and misery. As I mentioned at the premom stage, each one of my pregnancies was marked by four months of constant nausea. It was like the minute my body knew a human being was forming in there, I started having that nauseous feeling. It lasted for four months straight, vomiting four or five times per day. The only relief I got was when I was sleeping.

With Avery, my first son, of course, all this nausea was brand new, and there I was, a first-grade teacher. I felt I owed my young students some sort of explanation about why I looked so terrible and why I kept a trash can out in the hallway for regular vomiting sessions. After sending a note to the parents explaining my situation, I told the class, "There's a baby growing in my tummy, and Mrs. Tiras isn't feeling very good sometimes, so she has to go throw up in the hallway in the garbage can."

They handled it like champs. One student assured me that she knew all about it because her mom was pregnant and doing the same thing. Another wanted to know why I didn't have a big tummy. I had to explain that my tummy would get bigger as the baby grows ... then I rushed back out to the hallway to visit my trash can.

Most of us do not have the luxury of sleeping through this season of life. If you're working or you have other kids, your time is in demand, and you literally cannot take off. The best advice I can give you regarding nausea is to bear in mind that it will pass. Like many times in your motherhood career, you will gather your strength and push forward. The following five tips were given to me during my time of extreme "morning" sickness. I'll be straightforward: in my case none of these was very effective; however, many women do find relief with the following methods:

Tip #1 Stay Hydrated: When you're already feeling nauseous, the thought of eating or drinking anything can literally make things worse. Moreover your pregnant body doesn't really seem to care if you eat or drink, because you vomit regardless. Take my advice on this: do whatever you can to stay hydrated.

> **The best advice I can give you regarding nausea is to bear in mind that it will pass. Like many times in your motherhood career, you will gather your strength and push forward.**

During one pregnancy I was actually hospitalized because I was so dehydrated. The whole "saltine crackers and ginger ale" regimen did not cut it even one bit for me. The thing is we don't always realize that our hydration levels directly correlate to our levels of nausea. In the hospital they hooked me up to an IV for about half a day. The IV contained a saline solution, with the addition of glucose, dextrose, and electrolytes. Once I was fully hydrated, the nausea subsided, and I felt much better.

Tip #2 Eat Light—Eat Right: I found that the best way to manage nausea was to eat very small meals several times a day. Larger meals seemed to stagnate in the gut and eventually propelled back up. When I studied this, Healthline.com agreed with my conclusion! They suggest these tips for nausea in general:

- Eat something small every one to two hours.
- Eat and drink slowly and in small amounts.
- Do not lie flat after eating.
- Avoid food preparation.
- Keep your mouth clean.
- Avoid the following: fatty, greasy, or fried foods; very sweet foods; spicy foods; foods with strong odors; alcohol; caffeine.

Healthline.com goes on to list the following fourteen best foods to fight nausea:

- Ginger
- Water/clear beverages
- Crackers
- Pretzels
- Toast
- Cold foods
- Broth
- Bananas
- Applesauce
- Rice
- Potatoes
- Noodles
- Protein-rich meals
- Herbal tea

Tip #3 Nausea Bands: Many women find nausea relief with the use of nausea bands, also called nausea bracelets or sickness bands. Here's how blisslets.com describes the science behind sickness bands:

Nausea bands, also called nausea bracelets, trigger the P6 (Nei-Kuan or Nei-Guan) acupressure point, located slightly below the wrist on the underside of the arm, to relieve nausea from causes as diverse as motion sickness, morning sickness, chemotherapy, migraines, anesthesia, virtual reality, vertigo, and the flu. Some products apply pressure to the P6 point by means of a small bead or disk embedded in a snug-fitting band. Others zap this point with an electrical current.

If you're going to try nausea bracelets, one tip would be to carefully follow the instructions on the bands' packaging to make certain the pressure balls are placed accurately on the wrist. If they aren't, you will see zero relief.[3]

Tip #4 Doctor-Prescribed Medication: Doctor-prescribed medications help many pregnant women cope with nausea. At one point I was prescribed Zofran, which "works in the stomach to block the signals to the brain that cause nausea and vomiting."[4] Doesn't that sound like a wonderful thing? If you're really suffering with nausea, talk to your doctor about prescribing something to help.

EMOTIONAL? WHO? ME?

You may find yourself more emotional at the onset of pregnancy, and your hormones will likely cause emotional fluctuations throughout each trimester. Emotional flare-ups can hit you at any time, and you may feel you have no control over your reactions. Regrettably, I know about this from firsthand experience.

---

3   Blisslets, "The Complete Guide to Nausea Relief Bands," 2023, https://blisslets.com/blogs/the-blissblog/the-complete-guide-to-nausea-bands.

4   Mayo Clinic, "Drugs and Supplements: Ondansetron (Oral Route, Oromucosal Route)," last updated February 1, 2023, https://www.mayoclinic.org/drugs-supplements/ondansetron-oral-route-oromucosal-route/description/drg-20074421.

Remember the ovulation kits? I was so convinced they would work and that I was having a girl, I went to my ultrasound appointment decked out in pink. I'm sure I looked ridiculous: pink pants, pink shirt, pink socks, panties, and bra—everything pink!

Scott took me to my appointment; I was antsy and excited as we waited our turn, and we finally got called in for the ultrasound. The technician's eyes rounded a bit when he was assaulted by all the pink, but we chatted briefly, and he began the procedure.

As I was lying down on a cot, on went the ice-cold ultrasound gel; then the conversation: he said, "Do you want to know the sex of your child?"

Radiant, we replied, "Yes, yes! But we already know. It's a girl!"

The technician's face fell just a bit, and he added more ultrasound gel, bringing the scope around as if trying to be sure of what he was seeing. Then came these words: "No … you're having a boy."

This was where the hormonal emotions got the best of me. I mean I'd been eating the correct girl-producing foods; I had consistently been pinned upside down after sex; I was reading the book with all the answers; for the love of God, all of those ovulation kits … How could this go wrong? It was science!

There is a certain fire that can enter an expectant mother's eyes when she feels threatened—especially a hot-blooded Latina expectant mother—and that fire locked on to this poor technician. I recall him visibly shrinking back when I responded, "No! You need to look again because you're wrong!"

The technician turned the screen toward me, and there it was … biological proof that a boy was residing in my womb. I "couldn't" see it. Instead I lost my cool and yelled—loudly—demanding to see the head radiologist to provide a second opinion because he'd obviously made a mistake.

I could feel Scott next to me, squeezing my hand the whole time, and I could hear him trying to reassure me that everything would be okay. At that point, however, I had eyes only for the head radiologist, and there she was, providing another exam.

She assured me I was indeed having a very healthy baby boy and that there was every reason to be happy. When I wailed, even more upset, she focused my attention on the health of the baby. Then, of course, the emotional roller coaster that is pregnancy moved on to feeling bad about my reaction. There were so many women who wanted a child, and the real importance was that the baby was healthy and strong. Now I was crying again because I was happy that the baby was healthy and strong.

Afterward we went to pick up our boys at my friend Stacy's house, and I remember them running out, excitedly asking, "Mommy, Mommy, are we having a boy or a girl?"

I put this big smile on my face—as you will likely do a million times in your mothering career—and announced, "We're having a boy; we're gonna have our own little basketball team."

The emotions of pregnancy can be sporadic. My tip in dealing with them is to use your logical brain as much as possible to curb them—but truthfully, if we're truly being real, it rarely works.

HANG IN THERE ... THIS TOO SHALL PASS

Most women see a sharp decline in nausea and exhaustion at some point in their second trimester (four to six months). Typically, they've been watching their diet and taking prenatal vitamins throughout the first three months (if they were able), so oftentimes women feel better at this point than they've ever felt in their life.

For me the minute I finished my fourth month and started entering my fifth, the vomiting, dizziness, and sickness just disappeared. I was getting bigger in my belly, but it transferred into a feeling of cuteness: I had a baby bump!

NESTING IN THE FINAL MONTHS

Once pregnancy progresses and moms get past the majority of sickness, the anticipation of their new baby will start to take a practical turn. Something deeply instinctual will cause them to prepare their life for this event. Moms during this nesting phase typically feel driven to clean out closets, drawers, and old cabinets as if they're cleaning out an old life in order to prepare for the new calling of motherhood—which is exactly what is happening.

I of course wanted to get ahead of everything, and it's possible I obsessed just a bit—but many moms do! I discussed nesting details at length with other moms, read books on what to expect, and drew the conclusion that I wanted everything for the baby to be in its proper place when he arrived. I needed to focus on feeding, changing, and bathing the baby, then putting the baby to sleep—that's all.

Moms, I strongly suggest taking this approach. You don't want to worry about needing diapers or formula or a breast pump. Make sure, during your nesting phase, that you have everything you need for the baby's first several weeks. Make the baby's room ready for their arrival. Think about the baby's clothing for when they come home from the hospital—and don't forget the car seat! You must have the car seat installed properly, or the hospital staff will not release the baby.

LINEA NIGRA (THE PREGNANCY LINE)

An interesting manifestation that occurred with my pregnancies was the condition of a brown line appearing between the belly button and the pubic area.

This is what my.clevelandclinic.org says about this condition, officially known as linea nigra: "Linea nigra is a dark line that develops on your stomach during pregnancy. It usually extends from your bellybutton to your pubic area. The linea nigra is caused by an increase in hormones and fades once your baby is born."[5]

After all of the ups and downs, exhaustion, nausea, and significant body changes, being literally marked by pregnancy may be upsetting. Rest assured this condition goes away after you give birth.

DISCOMFORT IN THE LAST THREE MONTHS

Let's be straightforward here because there really is no way to sugarcoat it: the seventh through the ninth months of pregnancy are just plain uncomfortable. On top of this physical discomfort, emotionally you're waiting for your new life to start, and this can cause a certain restlessness or impatience.

Your new body is getting big, so much so that the pressure in your lower abdomen can be constant. Standing for long periods of time—or sitting for that matter—can cause painful spasms in areas you never before knew existed. Riding in a car can be very difficult as you try to contort your bulbous frame into the confines of the vehicle. Sleeping soundly is nearly impossible, as said pressure keeps you running to the bathroom all night long.

---

5   Cleveland Clinic, "Linea Nigra," last reviewed July 18, 2022, https://my.clevelandclinic.org/health/body/23488-linea-nigra.

Since I had a fairly rough time with discomfort, I found some ways to relieve the worst of it. Here are my four best tips for managing discomfort as you grow great with child:

Maternity Belt: As I mentioned, especially with my third and fourth pregnancies, the heaviness of the baby weighed down on the pelvic area. It's not so much "painful" as it is naggingly uncomfortable.

There is a special belt for this time, called a maternity belt. It's made with a large Velcro strap that slings underneath the belly and supports the weight.

My tip? Don't think twice; invest in one of these amazing belts.

Support Yourself: During the final three months too, the breast tenderness you've had throughout your pregnancy becomes more acute. Your breasts may be huge at this stage, and it almost feels like little rocks or cysts have been squeezed inside. The result, as you can imagine, can be painful.

When your baby is born, this pressure will naturally be relieved when the baby nurses. If you elect not to nurse, your doctor will provide instructions and medication to help dry up milk production. In the meantime invest in a good support bra. Everything—the back, legs, and breasts themselves—will feel better when the girls are well supported.

Regarding a support bra, my tip is to invest in a good nursing bra if you plan to nurse. A nursing bra is typically built to provide extra support while, of course, having a removable flap for breastfeeding. It made more sense to me to make one quality purchase in my ginormous pregnancy size since I'd never be that size again outside pregnancy.

Massage: I found that massaging the breasts relieves the pressure and tension, but massage in general can be hugely beneficial for overly strained muscles.

Many massage therapists specialize in massage that is targeted to expectant moms. I highly recommend finding a good chiropractor and massage therapist with a focus on pregnant women, and utilize this resource to the fullest extent.

Warm Shower: For those body aches and pains and also for that heightened breast tenderness, a warm shower can be greatly effective. Be prepared for breast leakage, as the water helps relax the breasts and relieve the pressure.

DELIVERY STAGE

Many moms feel very private about their delivery, and they allow only their husband/partner to be in the room with them. Other moms feel the occasion is something to celebrate, so they have many people involved in the birth. There is no right or wrong on this; do whatever you feel comfortable doing, of course, taking into consideration all hospital rules.

I was more of the mindset that a few of my closest family being present would only help Scott and me—especially if Scott fainted or something (I didn't know how he would react to this)! As I've already explained, I love photos and recording memories. For the birth of my children, I wanted all the raw, gruesome pictures: the cutting of the umbilical cord, the baby as the doctors first held him up, birth in all of its gory glory.

Going into my first delivery, I had everyone assembled, and they all knew their role in the delivery room. Scott was, of course, my coach. My dad was on camera detail—but he was restricted to my shoulder and head area only. My mom was coming in strong on video duty. All of them were sternly instructed not to go looking in the vaginal area. I mean I needed some privacy.

I have to back up and explain that, at this time in history, camera phones hadn't been invented. If we wanted something videotaped, we used a camcorder that was roughly the size of a small refrigerator. There was my five-foot-tall mother lugging twenty-five-plus pounds of camera over her shoulder, directly pointing at everything that was going on. We neglected to show her exactly how to use the camera, however, and in her zeal she did exactly what I instructed everyone not to do: she got way too close, and the camera was set to zoom. This threw the picture completely out of focus.

So the record of our first son's birth is a video of nothing—possibly a blob of my mother's forefinger, the floor, a leg, part of an ass cheek—but not of the birth! We're not making accusations since we truly never gave my mother instructions on how to even use the video camera. We don't know to this day whether it's funny or disturbing to view! Luckily my dad disobeyed just a bit at the most crucial time, and he got a great still photo of the actual birth and Scott cutting the umbilical cord.

As I said, each mom will judge for herself the amount of help needed in the delivery room. Following are my ten tips for delivery to add to your birthing toolbox. Pay special attention to numbers two and three.

Tip #1 As the Water Breaks: Like most new moms, with my first pregnancy, I didn't know what to expect. You can hear all the stories—moms love to tell their stories—but the birthing experience itself is unlike any other, and when it's happening to you, it's brand new.

There I was after a normal day, lying in bed trying to get to sleep. My due date was about five days away, so all good; right? Scott passed out in about eight seconds flat, as usual, and I was turning this way and that, trying to get comfortable. It was no use. I had the pillow between my legs, trying to align my hips and spine for relief, and that wasn't even working. I certainly couldn't sleep on my back at this point, as I wanted to, because that position created a whole different agony, like the baby was pressing down on all my organs.

On one particularly impatient flip to my other side, a gush of hot liquid suddenly escaped. God, did I just pee all over myself? A bit disoriented, I woke Scott up. He flew over to my side of the bed and flipped off the covers. What Scott saw amazed him. As I was lying on my side, holding my belly, there was a stream of liquid flying two feet in the air, like it was coming from a garden hose. The only way to stop it was to close my legs. Today, we understand that the position of the baby was causing this, but then, Scott and I observed this in bewilderment. Out of curiosity and fascination, I kept lifting a leg just to see if this hosing would continue.

Finally Scott made me get up, and he immediately started leading me toward the door. It was hospital time ... however, this was my first baby! I had to shower and put my makeup on, just as I would for any special event.

Tip #2 An Enema? You Bet! Okay, at this point we need to get very real about giving birth. Forget any TV show you've ever watched where, in full, undisturbed makeup and looking gorgeous, the heroine pushes and strains for thirty seconds, and a perfect baby emerges. That's a patently false image.

In real life the very same muscles used to poop are the ones used to push the baby out. I know one young woman who didn't understand this and pushed with her stomach muscles. She states that at one point nature took over, and she realized that birthing a child felt like the largest bowel movement possible. She's correct.

What do you think might go wrong when the bowel muscles are used? What will happen if that internal area isn't cleaned out? You guessed it, and many women have experienced it: you could poop on the table, right in front of your support team and all those doctors and nurses.

Luckily there is a solution to this horrifying dilemma: request an enema when you get to the hospital. I know seasoned moms who believed this was against typical hospital-care policies, but receiving an enema is absolutely something you can request upon admission to the hospital. Please don't expect the nursing staff to be thrilled with this request. They may even discourage it, and I'm sure what's required gives them good reason to discourage it. They will offer you water, ice chips, even a "cocktail," but they will not encourage an enema. If you want one, you must take control of the situation and ask for it directly.

Aside from not wanting to poop on the table with everyone present, I wanted to be cleaned out in case I was prescribed pain killers, as might happen with an emergency C-section. Medications are notorious for causing constipation, and the thought of being constipated, on top of the trauma that had just gone on down there, was something I did not want to experience. Better to clean out first, so there's nothing left to become constipated with.

Tip #3 I Need an Epidural ASAP! Oxford Languages defines an "epidural" as "an anesthetic used especially in childbirth to produce loss of sensation below the waist." I cannot think of anything better for the birthing experience. I made it known upon entry into the hospital that I wanted an epidural as soon as it was possible to give me one. I absolutely, 100 percent wanted a "loss of sensation below the waist."

Some women elect not to have an epidural because they fear they will lose out somehow on the birthing experience. This is, of course and as always, your

> **With an epidural, the only thing you miss out on is the pain.**

choice. However, here's my tip: with an epidural, the only thing you miss out on is the pain. You can still feel pressure; you're still taxed with the responsibility of pushing the baby out; and you're awake to greet this amazing new life into the world.

Tip #4 Transition: Like I said, I saw childbirth as a celebration, so our "party" assembled for my first delivery (mom, dad, Scott, me, the nursing staff, and Dr. Stanley Connor, who had delivered me as well as my first two boys, Avery and Ryan). The contractions began for real—no one understood the agony, except maybe my mother—and this "thing" came over me. "Mean" isn't quite the right word, but it was close!

Scott, like most young dads in his position, tried to soothe me with a gentle back rub or a reassuring pat to my arm, as if to say, "We're in this together!"

At the moment, I didn't see anyone in this but me, and he was the one who got me here, so "Don't touch me! No, I don't want juice or freaking ice chips! Don't look at me! Just get this thing out of me!"

Such is a typical reaction during transition, when a flood of adrenaline is released in the mother's body. Nature is preparing you for the final stage of childbirth.

Tip #5 Cocktails, Anyone? The doctor, at this point, thought it best to offer medication to calm me down. Through the IV this lovely "cocktail" washed through me, relaxing me, taking that sharp edge off.

Contractions were coming; I was doing my breathing; it was still so painful because the cocktail wasn't the epidural—it was the relaxing medication they give you before your epidural. The baby was starting to come; doctors and nurses were on it; everybody was there and handling their assigned tasks; Dad flipped off a few photos, and I wanted to smash the camera; my legs were open; they weighed about fifty pounds each, so Scott was holding one, and my mom was holding the other as if there were zero need for privacy.

With my pain level hitting fifteen out of a possible ten, the medical staff required me to remain perfectly still while they administered the epidural—no easy task! But then, oh, sweet relief; everything that hurt went numb. Once the epidural kicks in, the doctor must tell you when to push because you cannot feel it. The medical staff relies on the monitor to know when a contraction is coming.

Tip #6 Inducing Labor: Many women are faced with the prospect of inducing labor, sometimes in an emergency situation and sometimes planned. I don't have a long tale to tell about this, but my experience was so significant, I had to add it.

My first three deliveries were long and hard, taking everything out of me. Now I had three boys at home, so I was concerned about recovering quickly to care for them. It seemed it would be much easier to plan for something this life altering, so when the option of "inducing labor" was presented, I leapt at it.

I was scheduled to go in at two o'clock—hair and makeup all arranged, thank you very much. In went the IV of Pitocin, and out came my fourth son, Dawson.

Medical professionals will warn that because contractions build quickly and are stronger, inducing labor can be more painful. That was not my experience—mind you, this was my fourth child. My philosophy is that a stronger-but-shorter delivery time is better than hours of slow agony.

Tip #7 Delivering the Placenta: My God, Is It Twins? I read countless books about childbirth, and none of them explained the reality of delivering the placenta, also called the "afterbirth." This is something new moms need to be aware of! With my first delivery, I knew that there was a placenta and it needed to come out, but the process and the size of it were absolutely shocking.

Here I was, having just delivered; I hadn't even held the baby; I wanted to count his fingers and toes; I was oblivious to any other toil required on my part.

Dr. Connor tapped me on the knee and said, "I need you to focus on me now, and I need you to push."

I was like, "Oh, my God! Am I having twins?"

He said, "No; you need to push the placenta out."

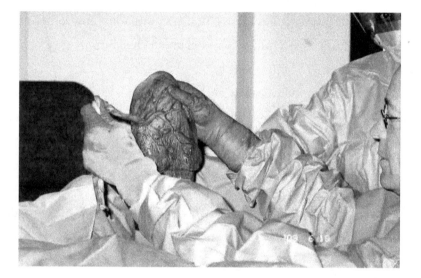

Avery's placenta.

Well, it may as well have been a twin by the size of it. As I said, I was stunned at the huge mass that was expelled. It came fast, just two or three pushes—and you bet your booties we got a picture of it!

Tip #8 The Episiotomy … They Do What? We're going to get very real again here because there are things that happen during delivery that are easier to handle if you know what's happening. The baby in the fetal position is similar in shape and weight to a youth's bowling ball. When this emerges, as you can imagine, the vagina can easily tear. Rather than allow that, the doctor will make a small incision at the base of the vagina to your butthole to more neatly accommodate the emerging child. That part was not in the brochure.

What no one tells you is that you can ask the doctor to sew you up as tightly as possible afterward. Why would we want to do that? Because when all is said and done, you want to have firmness in the vaginal area, if you know what I mean.

My tip on this one is to discuss tight stitching with your doctor prior to giving birth, and then remind them in the delivery room at the time of your episiotomy.

Tip #9 Complications at Birth: Most deliveries are noncomplicated and routine, but some can get scary, and moms have to trust their hospital staff to step in. It's the most horrifying and helpless feeling to give your child over to someone when they are in distress.

My third son, Reece's, delivery was one of those. First off, just prior to Reece's birth, my beloved Dr. Connor had been in a car accident and injured his hand. He eventually had to retire because of this, so he put me in the hands of his assistant, Dr. Schneider. When the time came for the baby to arrive, my team was with me at the hospital, and I could feel something going on in my body that seemed different from my other deliveries. The nurse had checked on me, and at that time I was only three centimeters dilated. Dr. Schneider was asleep, presumably in the doctor's lounge, and the nurse was very reluctant to wake him.

Back and forth we went, with me asking for the doctor, and the nurse telling me it wasn't time, and we could not call the doctor until the baby was actually coming.

At this point it was just me and my mom. Scott, amazingly, was asleep in a chair on the other side of the room. A few minutes after the nurse left, I looked at my mom and said, "I think the baby is coming out!"

When my mom looked, sure enough, the head was crowning. Everyone flew into action. Scott was off the chair and down the hall, calling for the nurse, within seconds; mom was at my shoulders, telling me to breathe; when the nurse came in, she did remain calm, as nurses are trained to do, but a split second of panic covered her face. She told me to refrain from pushing, which I did with great difficulty. When the doctor arrived a few minutes later, it was one, two, three pushes, and my son was born.

The trouble was he inhaled meconium, which is basically poop, during the delivery. Chaos was going on all around me, and all I wanted was to hold and protect that baby, but with concerned eyes bulging out over their masks, the medical staff whisked him away.

Tip #10 Follow That Baby! I want to assure you that Reece was absolutely fine. He had to stay in the ICU for about forty-eight hours, but he recovered and is a healthy young man today.

What happened when they took my son away like that was a blur of protective instinct came over me. The child wasn't tagged, so no one knew him outside that specific delivery room. I, his mother, hadn't even seen him yet!

Every hospital kidnapping that I had ever heard about ran through my head. Like Commissioner Gordon in the old Batman episodes, I looked at Scott, pointed at the door, and said, "Follow that baby!"

Scott saw the fierceness in my eyes, and as parents we connected. He bolted after the medical team and stayed with our son while my mom cared for me.

My goal isn't to plant fear in any mom, but my tip is this: if anyone tries to take your child anywhere before they are officially identified, have someone you trust stay with the baby to ensure they are properly identified.

VAGINAL BIRTH OR C-SECTION? THERE IS A CHOICE?

Okay, this one may seem out of place, like if we were going to discuss a choice in "how" to deliver, we should have already done so. I don't actually want to address it from the angle of medical choice. I want to address it from the very real perspective of how your intimate body will change with childbirth.

When I was a young mom, a trend of sorts had begun: moms were electing to have C-sections rather than deliver vaginally for the purpose of keeping that precious vaginal firmness intact. While that's valid (and there are times I wish I had gone that route!), my thinking was polar opposite.

I absolutely did not want to be scarred on my abdomen. Today, with medical and technological advancements, the C-section incisions are lower and create less tissue damage, but twenty-five years ago, the scar was prominent.

I remember Dr. Connor working with me through eighteen hours with my first son. I told him unless the baby was in distress, I wanted to deliver vaginally. The problem was that the baby had turned incorrectly. Every time I had a contraction, while I pushed, Dr. Connor would go in and turn the baby. It was agony.

My point to this is you do have a choice in the scars you take on in childbirth. Choose wisely.

• • •

I'm sure you can envision the sweetness coming your way: hours of gently rocking and nurturing this brand-new person, who you'll give everything for …

You will surely have those times during newbornhood, but this piece of reality should also be noted: a screaming infant is about to enter your world.

• • •

JOURNALING TIP FOR THE PREGNANCY STAGE

START THOSE BABY BOOKS!

Part of my nesting process was starting baby books—and again I highly recommend opening up the baby books and getting started before the newness of motherhood is upon you.

I started taking pictures of the nursery and the size of my belly. I recorded how I was feeling, what cravings I was having, what I was eating, and how much I weighed.

Journaling in this stage is a way of holding on to the moment and mentally preparing for what is coming, so moms and dads, start those baby books!

CHAPTER 3

NEWBORNHOOD

When my first son was born, it was "all the rage" to employ a maternity nurse to help new moms through that crucial first week or two of motherhood. I thought the service was fantastic, and my nurse, Sharon, was amazing. She taught me baby care: how to bathe the baby, burp him, change him, feed him, clean his tiny nose and ears, and most importantly she helped with feedings. Not only did she help me with the very new experience of breastfeeding and pumping, but she also used the pumped milk to feed the baby while I slept. If you're in a position to hire a maternity nurse for a few days after your baby comes home, I recommend it!

Since my son was one week early, Sharon was with another family, so of course my mom stepped in. The plan was to take turns staying up with the baby. We had every intention of carrying through on this, mind you, but that first night we were so in love, so mesmerized by "my first baby" and "her first grandchild" that we ended up staring at him and smelling him all night long. Warning: the love that consumes you when you look at and hold your baby will literally change your life.

Besides that bonding, the first three months—*at least!*—of caring for an infant consist of only four actions. You'll be absolutely astounded at how these duties—that's right, only four!—will consume your entire week, 24-7. Every moment of your existence will be consumed by carrying out these duties because the baby only does four things: cries, eats, poops, and sleeps. So your life will be centered around soothing the baby, feeding the baby, changing the baby, and managing sleep for the baby and yourself.

> **The first three months—at least!—of caring for an infant consist of only four actions.**

SOOTHING THE BABY

A relentlessly crying baby can be the most frustrating sound on earth to new parents. Your job is to care for the new bundle; you love her and want to be everything to her; yet you can't turn off that four-alarm screaming, no matter how you try. My heart, honestly, goes out to you if you're in this situation. I can tell you that, for the first three months of life, the baby can't fully look around and focus on things to entertain himself. When the baby is about four months, many moms report that the ability for the baby to reach, turn his head toward a sound, and entertain himself to some extent causes the "crying for no reason" to stop—thankfully!

During the first three months, be very aware of any type of medical problem that might be causing bouts of crying. Colic, "frequent, prolonged and intense crying or fussiness in a healthy infant"[6] can be a horrifying experience for both the baby and the parents. Your doctor can help you manage some physical and emotional stress that accompanies it.

If there is no medical reason for the baby to be crying, try making the atmosphere in your home very peaceful; use the classical music technique we'll talk about later in the chapter, under Managing Sleep for the Baby and Yourself; be sure the child feels very secure; check to see if the baby has spit up or needs another burp; give them love and attention and several minutes of reassurance; rock them and talk to them gently.

If the baby's needs are tended to and they continue to cry without reason, consider that the child should not rule the parents, and it's okay to let them cry. I am 100 percent Hispanic, and I believe in tough love. It's been my experience as a mom and a teacher that children feel most secure when clear boundaries are set. You actually establish the atmosphere of what is acceptable and unacceptable behavior, even with infants. I'm telling you now, I wasn't having screaming and crying in my home. I simply would not put up with it. My children came into this world knowing that, just as yours will automatically know where you draw the line.

Admittedly, "tough yet loving" is a difficult balance that all moms have to find. In the meantime you may still be dealing with a screamer. If that's your situation, again, bear in mind that many babies transform in that fourth month when they can see and entertain themselves, so hang in there. Keep reminding yourself that this stage is temporary.

If things get to be too much, use any or all the following tips from Healthline.com to try to rest and realign yourself.

---

6   Mayo Clinic, "Colic, Symptoms and Causes, Overview," April 5, 2022, https://www.mayoclinic.org/diseases-conditions/colic/symptoms-causes/syc-20371074.

Setting aside time to practice self-care may help reduce your stress levels. Practical examples include the following:

- Going for a walk outside
- Taking a bath
- Lighting candles
- Reading a good book
- Exercising
- Preparing a healthy meal
- Stretching before bed
- Getting a massage
- Practicing a hobby
- Using a diffuser with calming scents
- Practicing yoga[7]

FEEDING THE BABY

Besides physical nourishment, feeding your infant is, and should be, a bonding experience. You'll find your little bundle watching you closely when they can focus; they'll coo and smile at you as they get a bit older; and you'll never forget the first time your baby reaches to touch you. My best tip is to turn the TV off and silence your phone during feedings. In fact put it on the other side of the room. Take this time to interact fully with your newborn. It honestly does not matter if you breastfeed or bottle-feed; what matters is spending that time interacting with the baby.

At the time of this writing, the world is experiencing a formula shortage, and moms are making decisions regarding breast- or bottle-

---

7   Jillian Kubala and Kerri-Ann Jennings, "15 Simple Ways to Relieve Stress," updated January 20, 2022, https://www.healthline.com/nutrition/16-ways-relieve-stress-anxiety.

feeding purely for practical reasons. My sister-in-law is in this predica-
ment right now, expecting her baby in just a few months. The interesting
thing is that my brother, Alan, automatically concluded that breastfeeding under these extreme circumstances is the answer. Although his
conclusion is sensible, I warned him against that assumption.

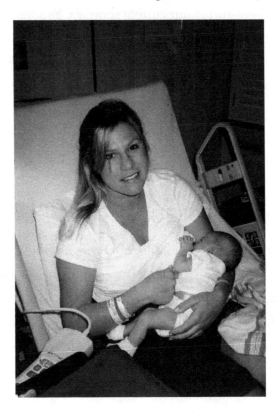

Jenn nursing Dawson.

Personally I loved the breastfeeding experience, and I felt it was
easier than the process my bottle-feeding comrades had to go through,
but it's really not for everyone. Sometimes the new mom can't produce
enough milk for the baby; some moms have inverted nipples, and
the baby latches on better to the bottle; and some moms work, and
they find that pumping and keeping up with all the other demands
of newbornhood is too overwhelming.

If any situation or personal, emotional conflict limits you and you choose not to breastfeed, refuse to internalize any negative feelings. Simply focus on making feeding time a special, bonding experience, no matter how it's done.

If you'll be bottle-feeding, think very clearly about your formula choices, especially during our current shortage. You want to take into consideration your child's tolerance for certain formulas when making your selection. Some babies have allergies and digestive sensitivities to take into account. Also, some formulas claim to be better because they are plant based. Sounds good, right? Do your research. Plant-based formulas aren't necessarily "natural," and they contain additives you likely want to avoid.

NIGHTTIME FEEDING

Feeding your infant in the middle of the night, when you're barely functioning, may be one of the not-so-joyous parts of motherhood. Some moms manage this difficult time by putting the baby in bed with them, feeding them there while the mom lies on her side, and letting the baby sleep between the parents. Although this may seem easier at first, oftentimes parents don't sleep peacefully for fear of rolling onto the child and smothering them, a legitimate concern!

Because my husband had to get up early for work, as soon as I heard the baby on the monitor, I'd turn it off and head straight to the baby's room. The whole process of feeding, burping, changing, and putting the baby back to sleep was necessary when handling night feedings. Why? Because the baby was resettled and ready for sleep. Then I would slip back into my bed, and everyone rested soundly.

BURPING THE BABY

My final thoughts on feeding are centered around the necessity of burping the baby. Babies swallow air during feedings, and this air must be released. Your medical team will show you different burping positions, typically over your shoulder or sitting the baby up on your lap. As a mom who's been there, my two tips for burping are as follows:

Have a Cloth Handy: If there is spit-up or mess to deal with—and you'll be surprised at the messes!—you want to have a cloth for cleanup ready to go.

The Baby Won't Break: In order to release the painful air buildup in your baby's belly, you need to apply enough pressure as you pat the baby's back to elicit a burp. It's quite a firm pressure, and I assure you the baby won't break! That said, if you have any concerns about how firmly to pat your baby during burping, speak with your doctor or lactation professional.

READ TO YOUR NEWBORN

You may wonder how exactly to "interact" with a newborn, and reading to them is one of the best ways you can do that. Try reading to your child during feedings. Admittedly you're not going to see huge interaction from a tiny baby, but the fact is you're communicating with and focusing on your infant, and they know it. Stimulate your child's brain by using animated voices and tones; enjoy the story and experience.

I had everyone in the family reading to the kids, and it was a newer thing for my mom and my husband. Especially if they were giving the kids their night bottle, I'd have them read to the boys. This practice established a definite routine of reading in our home. (Interesting note: all our sons became avid readers.)

My tip: read, read, read, and read more to your children!

MILK PRODUCTION ASSISTANCE

As your baby suckles, a trigger is set off in the brain to produce more milk to accommodate the baby's continued growth. In some cases, like my own, the body just can't produce enough milk, no matter how much the baby suckles. In the earliest months of our babies' lives, I was able to produce enough to satisfy my infants, but as they grew and demanded more, it just wasn't there. I was determined to nurse each one for six months, so this sent me on a quest to find ways to produce more milk.

Organic Mother's Milk tea, by Traditional Medicinals, seemed like an easy, sound solution. It has all kinds of herbs associated with lactation. I can't remember if it worked, but I do remember that drinking it brought on constant body odor! I smelled like some sort of rotten spice. It was gross, frankly, but I forged ahead.

The two tactics I do recall being effective were 1) drinking a lot of water, and 2) getting plenty of sleep. I found I had to be careful when supplementing with formula because I wanted the baby to feed off me to get that brain-producing chemistry into high gear.

If you're having trouble with milk production but want to continue nursing, it's essential that the baby nurse as much as possible.

MASTITIS AND CRACKED NIPPLES

Mayoclinic.org provides this overview of the painful condition some breastfeeding moms experience, known as "mastitis":

Mastitis is an inflammation of breast tissue that sometimes involves an infection. The inflammation results in breast pain, swelling, warmth, and redness. You might also have fever and chills.

Mastitis most commonly affects women who are breastfeeding (lactation mastitis). But mastitis can occur in women who aren't breastfeeding and in men.

Lactation mastitis can cause you to feel run down, making it difficult to care for your baby. Sometimes mastitis leads a mother to wean her baby before she intends to. But continuing to breastfeed, even while taking an antibiotic to treat mastitis, is better for you and your baby.[8]

Unfortunately, I fought through this condition with my first son, which resulted in cracked nipples. The second, third, and fourth breastfeeding experiences were smooth, and I did not have either condition, so I assume my body had adjusted. An antibiotic was prescribed for the infection, and an ointment was given for the cracked nipples. The process was to allow the baby to nurse off the uninfected breast. I wondered if that was safe, and my doctor assured me it was.

The breast that was infected had to be pumped, and the milk had to be thrown away. "Wasting" any breast milk was painful on another level because, as I mentioned, I didn't have an overly generous milk supply, or as we called it "liquid gold." It nearly killed me every time I had to throw milk away, but that's what is needed when dealing with a mastitis infection.

If you experience this awful condition, follow your doctor's or lactation expert's advice on treatment. The most effective tip my

---

8   Mayo Clinic, "Mastitis, Symptoms and Causes, Overview," September 13, 2022, https://www.mayoclinic.org/diseases-conditions/mastitis/symptoms-causes/syc-20374829.

doctor gave me was the warm-shower method of allowing the water to relax the breast area in order to release the plugged ducts.

CHANGING THE BABY

The only thing to say about changing diapers is it's gross, so plan now to potty train your child early. (We'll discuss potty training at length in the next chapter!)

My tips on changing the baby are really very practical:

1. **Always keep the baby in a clean diaper:** This will save you a world of hurt trying to deal with and get rid of diaper rash later.

2. **Fit the diaper on the body firmly:** Again, the baby will not break. You don't want gaps left around the legs or in the back where messes can escape.

3. **For boys specifically:** When the diaper is removed and air hits the penis, this stimulates a stream of new urine coming straight at you. On more than one occasion, I was hit directly in the eye with this wayward stream, and I learned to *have tissues readily available.* The soiled diaper comes off, the tissue is immediately put over the penis to catch the stream, and all is well.

There is a product designed for this purpose, called a "Pee-pee Teepee." These are cone-shaped, absorbent cloths that are able to be washed and reused. Pretty nifty idea, if you ask me.

BATHING THE BABY

Part of changing the baby is bathing the baby. Whether you have an infant bath seat or you cradle the baby directly in the kitchen sink, safety is my biggest tip.

When Reece (our third son) started walking, we had a bathtub scare that causes "safety" to blaze like a neon sign in my brain for all stages. The reason this was so scary is because it started out so normal; all the bath planning had been tended to just like any other day.

Reece was lifting his leg to get out of the tub, and his foot slipped. All his weight came crashing down onto his chin as it hit the edge of the tub. Blood gushed from the bottom of his chin, and we thought he had seriously injured himself. After several chaotic, bloody moments, thankfully we discerned that he would likely have a fat lip, but he was okay.

Bath safety is critical, and it begins with the very first bath. Here are my best bath-time tips:

1. Don't leave them alone, no matter their age, for even a second.

2. Have everything you need—washcloths, toys, towels, clean clothing, and any miscellaneous items—ready and handy.

3. Use a bathtub safety seat to stabilize them as they're learning to sit by themselves.

4. As they get older, use bubbles, food coloring, or shaving cream to make bath time fun. This is a great time to teach them about colors, textures, and different scents.

5. When they can safely sit up and play, and especially if they have another sibling to play with, bring yourself some enter-

tainment, seeing as you'll need to be supervising. I took this time to make my grocery list, write my "to dos," and take care of calls that needed attention while keeping a close eye on the kids.

SHOWERING WITH THE BABY

Some parents get a little squeamish about this, but honestly simply bringing the baby into the shower with you and just getting the job done can be both practical and bonding.

If you go this route, safety is still my biggest tip. Infants' skin is so soft that the baby can easily slip out of your hands when wet. Mesh baby carriers are available to assist in holding the baby, and they can be ideal for the shower. If you don't have a mesh carrier, use a towel or washcloth over your arm to provide a good grip on the child.

I've had moms who love this method of bathing ask me when the appropriate time is to stop showering with the baby. The simple answer to that is, "When they become aware." For me, my son innocently grabbed my boob one day and asked, "What's that?"

Moms, you'll perfect this sort of calm-mom voice when you're really panicking, and with that voice, I answered, "That's called a boob, and we're not going to touch it." We finished our shower without further incident, but that was the last shower I took with any of our boys. I told Scott it was his turn—Mama is out.

Some kids become aware very young, and some are totally innocent all through their toddler years, so a certain age is impossible to state. You'll just know at one point it's time for them to shower alone.

MANAGING SLEEP FOR THE BABY AND YOURSELF

Hands down the most talked-about difficulty of raising an infant is managing sleep for the baby and the mom. As we've already discussed, you'll be shocked at how only four basic needs will keep you in a constant state of planning, preparing, and busyness. For you to tap into your best parenting instincts, it's critical that you be rested. For that to happen, the baby needs to sleep. Here are my best tips for getting the baby to sleep and stay asleep:

Tip # 1 Turn the Music Up! From the first day you bring your new infant home, put them in the crib, and play Mozart, Beethoven, and other classical music. This technique, along with being hugely beneficial for the brain and the synapses, automatically trains your child that when the music goes on, they go off to sleep.

During the first three months, when they sleep the majority of the day, keep the music on as gentle background "noise" as much as possible.

As they grow and begin to be more aware, start playing this music as you prepare them for bed. They see you're shutting the curtains; the sun is going down; they're having their bath; and the classical music is preparing them for sleep.

As they get a bit older, the routine may change slightly; maybe you read them a story or have prayer or conversation time, all while this gentle music is playing.

During daytime naps turn that music up! Then, when the doorbell is ringing with the Amazon shipment and the dog starts barking and the phone is buzzing, your child—even when they're older and could be done with napping—is safely off in la-la land. Why? Because they're trained that classical music means "sleep time."

If your child is unable (or unwilling) to sleep for that amount of time, this method still trains them that this is "quiet time." Perhaps the child doesn't necessarily sleep, but during this time, when the classical music is on, we're going to give our brain and body a rest.

This time is important for you as well, and you should never be sorry for taking it. Like many of you, I didn't have a housekeeper or nanny when we were first starting out. Nap time was when I took a shower, made dinner for the night, returned messages, made phone calls—whatever—it was my time, and it was necessary.

Recently, Avery and I were at the mall, and the shop we were in had classical music playing. I was stunned when my son looked at me with a thoughtful expression and said, "I think this was one of the songs you used to play when I took a nap." Yes, in fact, it was! It's embedded in his brain, and he can likely still use this technique for sleeplessness as an adult, if necessary.

Tip #2 Sleep When the Baby Sleeps. You'll hear this phrase a lot, and it is absolute wisdom to sleep when the baby sleeps during the first four to six weeks when a routine is being established. Carrying through on that, though, may require unexpected discipline. What typically happens when the baby falls asleep is that you have some time to yourself, and there are a million things to do! How can a new mom just sleep?

I remember that by the time I was done feeding, burping, and changing the baby—twice because it was common for some sort of mess to occur—I would no sooner finish this cycle when it was time to start it again! If you don't sleep when the baby is sleeping, you may not be rested at all. Handling the demands of a newborn in a state of constant sleep deprivation will not bring out your best parenting abilities. Be sure to prioritize your sleep!

Tip #3 Teach the Baby to Self-Soothe. I was never one to put the baby in the car and ride around the neighborhood to get them to sleep. The baby has to revolve around my schedule. I'm not going out of my way to create the perfect sleeping atmosphere for every child in the house. They just need to figure out how to go to sleep.

If that means letting them cry once their needs are met, then allow them to cry. You're actually teaching them the critical step of self-soothing, learning how to get themselves back to sleep.

Tip #4 Reminder! Say "Yes" to Help! If you're spending every waking moment taking care of the baby's four needs, and you're sleeping when the baby sleeps, you can only imagine the number of things that may pile up. Remember in the premom stage when I suggested lining up your help? This is why it's necessary!

We're not talking about a lifetime of people invading your space, but for the first four to six weeks, help is needed to get you back on your feet and comfortably in a routine. Having meals already prepared or having someone straighten your house or give you a few minutes of downtime while they care for the baby is necessary. Don't be shy about it, and don't try to be Superwoman at this time. All your strength will be needed for the parenting journey ahead of you, so allow yourself to get off on the right foot by accepting the help you need.

THE IMPORTANCE OF THE INFANT ROUTINE

Consistency is the key to your sanity when it comes to parenting, and it starts in newbornhood. The first four to six weeks of trying to figure everything out will progress into identifiable patterns, such as "Avery wakes every morning at 5:20; Reece is most awake during the midmorning hours; Ryan naps most soundly during the afternoon."

A routine is beginning to form. You can, and absolutely should, guide this routine into one that suits you as the parent.

Use the classical music technique to dictate sleep when you need it. Exhaust the child by keeping them up as much as possible. Move the infant's legs and arms; engage them by talking, singing, and playing. Eventually the child will be alert enough to keep awake on their own, but for now they need some help.

Consistency is the key to your sanity when it comes to parenting, and it starts in newbornhood.

When you're ready for the baby to sleep, put the classical music on, bathe them, immediately feed them, and likely as not, at this point they'll be out cold. The minute they are put to bed, run for your own! Prepare yourself for bed quickly and get to sleep because the baby will be up again in three hours, and the cycle starts all over.

• • •

I want to reiterate that it's imperative that you take care of yourself throughout your mothering journey in order to be the best mom you can be. There's nothing glamorous about mothering an infant; it can, quite honestly, feel gross. If they aren't suckling at your breast, they find your neck, your shoulder, whatever they can to drool or spit up on. You're literally dealing with a tiny person's bodily fluids all day long. There is no guilt or shame in getting away for a while to care for yourself.

• • •

Just when you get a handle on this phase, when you become an expert at juggling a baby and performing every other task in life with one hand, they grow and change, causing you to adjust again. If you thought the newborn stage was challenging, in the next they can move of their own volition—and they're lightning fast! Welcome to the toddler stage.

• • •

JOURNALING TIP FOR NEWBORNHOOD

WHAT SHOULD I WRITE ABOUT?

Hopefully you've already opened your baby books and gotten started on some of your mommy journaling. Even so you may wonder what to journal about. Here are a few partial entries from my first journals, just to give you some ideas:

- Today is Avery's six-month birthday, and he has grown and changed in every way possible ...
- Avery, I am watching you run, talk, splash, and play in the backyard. You are a ball of fire in my eyes, and I love you so much. You have taught me so much as a person and a mother.
- Ryan turned seven months and has been crawling since he was five-and-a-half months. He pulls up anywhere he can and always wants to be on the go.
- Ryan has been saying "dada" and "adada." He is a very quiet baby when he plays, and he's fascinated with all his big brother's toys.

- Ryan, at seven months, still has no teeth, but we still give him Cheerios—we love you!
- Reece: When Reece gets tired, he sucks his left thumb while holding his green "NiNi" (lovey), and with his right hand he strokes Kally's fur [dog]. Sweet moments!
- Reece: "Fang Baby" we call him because he is our first baby to show his upper canines.
- Reece is nine months, and so far he's eaten dog food, stirred toilet water, eaten bird poop and plant dirt. He is so quick, we call him "Frito Bandito."
- Reece is ten months and can wave "bye, bye." And for the first time, at Jax Grill, he waved bye and said, "bye." He loves balls and throws them to you.
- Dawson is one week old, and I am changing his diaper on the kitchen counter. He sprays pee in the air like a water fountain. Daddy's jaw drops in amazement.
- Dawson is five weeks old with a double chin. We cannot figure out who he looks like. We absolutely love Baby D!
- Dawson, at five months old, started holding his bottle and clearly understands "tuto" and "papa." He loves sucking his left thumb and watches Reece constantly.
- Dawson is six months old. He is babbling "dada" and blowing raspberries. If left on the floor, he scoots around. Also sitting up on his own quite well.
- Dawson is nine months old and crawling. He loves to tackle anyone lying on the floor. He bites hard and pulls your hair.

As you can see, the answer to "What should I write about?" is to record any memory, feeling, or observation that means something to you.

CHAPTER 4

THE TODDLER YEARS

Fair warning, you have entered the speediest, most exasperating, and most adorable time of motherhood. In this stage you will develop a keen sixth sense. What you can't see you can hear; and what you can't see or hear you will miraculously be able to feel. Silence will send you into a panic; you are part psychic, part planner; and in a noisy room you can pick out the slightest sounds of distress from your child. You move like lightning and have an uncanny way of knowing the types of trouble any new environment can create. Your eyes are everywhere; you're growing into your mommy superpowers.

If this sounds exhausting, it is. This stage requires constant awareness of your child and their actions. You have entered the toddler stage.

EVERY MOMENT IS A TEACHABLE MOMENT

One of your superpowers will undoubtedly be in communicating with your child. No one knows them like you do, so when you speak to them, respect them at the level they are at. What in the world do I mean by that?

At the toddler level, every single thing is new. So "speaking to your child at their level" means making even the simplest moments teachable. "Why do you think the dog is upset? Do you remember what color the cat was on page three? Let's count the steps as we go down: one, two, three."

Taking your child to the grocery store can be a learning experience every time. Allow them to put the apples in the bag; count as you go; discuss which ones look red and which ones look green. It takes a bit longer, so you want to plan for this. (If you're in a rush, a child fumbling with the apples will have a nonproductive effect.)

As an educator and mom, I've seen children who are engaged with and spoken to in this way leaping past those who aren't treated with this type of respect in their interactions. Make every moment teachable by talking to them at their level.

MORE BOOKS, *PLEASE!*

I was extremely lucky to work as a teacher for two years before becoming a mom. As such, I was eligible for awards through the Scholastic Book Club when my students hit certain benchmarks for book sales. I was getting five to ten brand-new books every month, by great authors like Eric Carle.

At the toddler stage, I might read five books to my boys in one sitting, and we always read during the bedtime routine. If the book was very long, sometimes we would stop partway through and pick up the next night, but there was always reading going on. In fact I had "book baskets" all over my house: there was a bathroom book basket, kitchen book basket, parents-bedroom book basket (for the weekend mornings when they climbed into bed with us), and I was deliberate about changing out the books, so there was always something new in them.

Now that my sons are older, I replaced the books with my Shutterfly journals, so now we enjoy great memories whenever we can.

Once I stopped teaching and I did not have those books coming in, it became a question of how to maintain fresh reading material. These were my go-to solutions:

1. **The Local Library:** As my kids got older, I had books, but none that was at their developing age levels, so we went to the library regularly. It was somewhat of a special day for us, actually, and I suggest making "library day" a fun event in your home.

2. **Book Swaps:** Many moms, understanding the importance of reading, have quite the library. A group of moms I met with regularly decided to share their libraries, and we started a book swap. It was a wonderful way to expand our access to great books.

My tip for this would be to have everyone clearly mark their names in the books, and be conscientious about returning them to their owners in a timely fashion.

If you don't have a mom group with a great book selection for your child's age and interests, look into some online book swaps, like ReadingRockets.org. With resources like this, there's almost no limit to the amount of quality books you can obtain for your child.

ELECTRONIC DEVICES

I want to be very clear regarding electronics: I absolutely, 100 percent, disagree with plunking a child down in front of a computer or television screen for hours on end.

However, technology is here to stay, and I think having "computer time," where actual learning is taking place for thirty to forty-five minutes, is highly productive.

Avery had a LeapPad, which is similar to an iPad, except it was brightly colored and preloaded with learning games for kids. At the age of two, he could name all the states because of the game he played on his LeapPad.

Electronic devices keep kids occupied because they have a mesmerizing (zombie-like) effect on them. Use real books, crayons, and finger paints whenever possible to stimulate the toddler brain. Limit the time, and certainly the programs, you permit on electronic devices.

POTTY TRAINING

Several years ago Scott and I were on vacation in Arizona, and we got to talking to a few other parents over breakfast. One mom was having some frustration because her nearly-three-year-old showed no signs of being ready to use the potty. When I began to explain my strategy for potty training, her eyes were glued to me, taking in every word.

Similar situations happen to me all the time, where one minute I'm going about my day and the next I'm discussing parenting strategies. Of all the subjects that young moms want to learn about and need simplified, it's the subject of potty training. Here is my eight-step strategy for successful potty training:

1. **You, the Parent, Must Be Ready:** *Many* unsuccessful potty-training attempts happen because the parent trainer isn't actually ready for the commitment training takes. This isn't a judgment on those parents; it's a simple caution to hold off training until the time is right for you. As we get into the steps, you'll see that some time off and rock-solid determination are necessary to successfully complete potty training. You cannot start and stop, or the child will be confused, and both of you will be frustrated.

2. **Start Planting the Seed:** Be sensitive to the newness of using the potty. Avoid creating an atmosphere of dread around the issue by preparing the child for this change. While shopping, say something like, "Oh, there's the big-boy/girl underwear. These are so cool. I can't wait 'til we don't have any more diapers and you can wear this superhero underwear." Make this a big deal, something positive to look forward to.

3. **Start Counting:** When you're at home, start counting down the diapers. "Oh, there are twenty diapers ... now we have fifteen diapers ... five ... we only have three diapers left ... we don't have any more diapers!"

   You're obviously timing this so that the day there are "no more diapers," you're prepared to stay home an entire day—maybe two—and spend it focused only on potty training. This won't be the day to get your nails done or visit playgroups; this is potty-training day, and all you will be doing is potty training.

4. **Let Them Pick Their Underwear:** Letting the toddler select their new big-boy/girl underwear is part of the process of

building it up. We would take a regular trip to the store, and I'd say something like, "Ooh, what cartoon character do you want to get when you're in your big-boy underwear? Because we're running out of diapers, and you'll be in big-boy underwear soon. We need to figure out, are we getting Spiderman or Superman?" Make it really fun, but be sure they don't wear the new underwear until potty-training day. *Make sure the **new underwear** is in the house on potty-training day, along with **stickers** and sheets of **construction paper or poster board**.*

5. **Potty-Training Day Lockdown:** The final process is to stay home, hang out, and play games with your child all day long. I used to take my son's shirt off and put him in his new superhero underwear, then give him sippy cups of water to drink all day long. If you have to take sips from your own cup to encourage drinking, go ahead and make a game of it. Then, every thirty minutes, take them to the potty.

    When they successfully go pee, let them select one sticker; if they poop in the potty, let them select two stickers. Allow them to place their stickers anywhere on their paper to create their very own potty chart. Display their potty chart in the house, proudly making a fuss over their achievements.

    Here are a couple of examples of potty charts from my boys.

Avery's potty chart.

Reece's potty chart.

6. **Keep It Positive—Always:** Whenever you're dealing with a child, you will find it more productive to turn the situation from a negative to a positive.

   So avoid this: "If you misbehave in the store, you won't get a toy."

   Instead, try this: "If you stay quiet and keep your hands inside of the cart/seat, we can get a small toy on the way out."

   Avoid this: "Pick up this room, or we're not going to Grandma's."

   Try this: "Guess what? As soon as all the toys are picked up, we can leave for Grandma's house!"

   With potty training, it's the same concept: "When you go pee on the potty, you get one sticker, and if you poop on the potty, you get *two* stickers!"

   Never remove a sticker that they successfully earned. If mistakes are made, they don't earn a sticker in that case, but turn it back around to a positive quickly: "As soon as all your stickers are earned, we can go get a toy!"

7. **Don't Rush to Clean Them Up:** If accidents happen, the consequence really should be the discomfort they feel in big-kid underwear. Let them feel the discomfort, smell the odor, and deal with the foulness involved with an accident. If you have to throw away a new pair of superhero underwear, so be it. Do not make it easy by using disposable underwear, and they'll decide all on their own that this is unwanted.

8. **Reward Day:** Be prepared for reward day because this will take their potty-training success to the next level.

When they've successfully earned about twenty stickers, take them and their sticker sheet to the store and have them "turn in" their chart for one store item. Tip: we kept it small and went to a dollar store!

You may have to explain a bit to the staff while you slip them the actual money: "Reece is turning in his potty-training stickers because he did pee-pee in the toilet. Now he's buying these little toy soldiers." The cashiers always played along and got a kick out of the process.

I've used this method with all four of my boys. It took about a week each, and all four were out of diapers by eighteen months old. It's all based on positive reinforcement and being prepared. Obviously, later on they're not going to go every thirty minutes, but for that first day, you're really training their brain to be aware of their urge and go on the potty. After a while it just becomes automatic; the chart and reward fall away, and the child is trained.

NIGHTTIME TRAINING

For nighttime, my training method was basically three steps, but admittedly this does require commitment on the parents' part. Once again make sure you're ready and have the time (and strength!) to train.

1. Stop all fluids by six o'clock in the evening, and encourage the child to go as much as possible before bedtime.

2. Before you go to bed, or around eleven o'clock, very gently "wake" them, take them to the potty, then guide them back to bed.

Parents are sometimes horrified at this thought. They spent two hours getting the toddler to sleep; there's no way they're waking them up! Be assured most children are typically so drowsed out that they go right back to sleep.

3. For about a week, set an alarm for 3:00 a.m. or so, and take them again. Just like before, when they are done, everyone goes back to sleep. Eventually they get the hang of holding it until morning without this motivation.

- One very practical nighttime tip is to purchase plastic covers for your child's mattress. Accidents do happen, and you want to protect the mattress (and your sanity!) from any long-term damage.

ACCIDENTS HAPPEN

Never believe that you'll remember. Assume you'll forget, and write it all down!

Moms and dads, your patience may be tested to the limit, but try to be very understanding about accidents or any type of illness that may cause a child to lapse in their training. Keep things light, and laugh together with your child whenever possible.

One day, when Avery was a toddler, we were in the car when he informed me that he had to poop. (Yikes; please, not in my vehicle!)

I said, "Okay, we will be at playgroup in a few minutes; squeeze your cheeks together and hold on!"

When I looked in the rearview mirror, he was holding his face and squishing his cheeks together. He looked like a determined little fish. I had to laugh with him and try to explain, "Not those cheeks—your butt cheeks."

The lightheartedness, thankfully, distracted him, and we made it to playgroup in the nick of time. (This was one of those journal entries that I probably would have forgotten ever happened if I hadn't written it down. Never believe that you'll remember. *Assume you'll forget, and write it all down!*)

PLAYGROUPS—THEY'LL SAVE YOUR SANITY!

Let me start this off with a true story that happened within a week of writing this: I had the privilege over summer to meet an eight-year-old boy who was participating in a summer camp. This young man was very polite, smart, and goodhearted; however, he was "different" from the other kids. He was quieter, and he was more apt to watch the activities rather than participate in them.

I immediately assessed that this child was either an only child or he had much older siblings. It was obvious that he was mostly in the company of adults. Turns out, in conversation one morning, he confirmed that this was exactly the case: he had older siblings who were already adults.

Here was the problem: while I understood him, the other children did not. He wasn't bullied in any way, but no matter how the counselors tried to include him, he ended up left out. He couldn't seem to make a good connection with any of the other campers. This wasn't because the other children were mean but because none of them could find any common ground to connect on. It was very sad to witness, and in the end he did not complete the camp.

This is an example of a nonsocialized child, and as social media and internet games abound, this type of lack in development becomes the norm for more and more children every day. Why?

Let's say a three-year-old is playing a game on his iPad, nice and quiet for most of the afternoon; his mom even brags about how easy she's got it. During the game, a character falls down and skins his knee—harmless enough, right? What does the child do about it?

Nothing. There is nothing to do. Does he empathize with that character? Not at all. In fact he may laugh at the way the character fell, or he may be angry because he lost points in the game because the "stupid character" fell down. He restarts the game, and all he has learned, quite honestly, is selfishness.

Now take that same child and put him in a group of children. Granted, the noise level is higher and his mom has way more to do to keep his behavior in check because he's interacting with other playmates, but her child is making friends! Now when his best little friend falls down and scrapes his knee, it's a whole different experience. All play likely stops for several minutes while the wound is tended to; the child's best friend is hurt, so he has the opportunity to learn compassion; mom, this is your chance to step in and allow your child to grow in self-worth by suggesting he help the friend, perhaps run to get Band-Aids, or sit quietly with them until they feel better.

Do you see the difference in the learning experience? The whole being of the child with a playmate becomes engaged. Children are meant to have this interaction; it's a necessary part of development, and playgroups were my go-to way of bringing it to my children.

HOW DOES PLAYGROUP WORK?

So that everyone knows the etiquette, playgroup is a parent-and-baby activity. Moms and/or dads attend playgroup with the kids. It would be a noticeable faux pas to try to leave your child as if the other playgroup parents are babysitters.

That said, playgroup really starts with gathering a group of other parents with kids close in age to yours. (Remember all those nice families from the childbirth class?) We would meet at someone's house every week, and we'd rotate houses so no one became overwhelmed. When the kids were tiny, we basically visited, had snacks or lunch, and supported each other.

As the babies began to crawl, we'd sit in a big circle and let them move freely and play with toys. The host mom was in charge of disinfecting the toys, as, of course, toys go straight in the mouth at this age.

When the children got older still, we would take them on outings, like trips to the zoo, the museum, or the rodeo. We went strawberry picking, took them to various parks, and at one point we all signed up for Gymboree together.

This became a real social group—like a second family. We celebrated each other's birthdays and shared life together, and the kids are still friends today. In fact Dawson's best friend is a young man he grew up with in playgroup. He is like my fifth son, and he's spending the day at our house today.

PLAYGROUP ACTIVITIES

Activities such as arts and crafts, playing sports, and going on different learning enrichment outings stimulate the toddler brain. Encourage your playgroups to do all this and more!

If you're shy, all it takes is showing up to playgroup with your child. From there, opportunities to participate will form. If you're that very social mom, your skills may be needed to organize activities.

However you manage it, be sure your kids are active. Take the electronics away during the toddler time of life, and let their brains grow by having enriching experiences.

LOTS OF TOYS FOR GIRLS AND BOYS

Another huge benefit of playgroup is the number of new and stimulating toys each child gets to enjoy by rotating houses. Young children become bored with their own toys quickly, but if there are four other families sharing toys during playgroup, they have different creative stimulation with each household's toys.

Better still, when playgroup comes to your house, your kids get a renewed interest in their own toys while playing with other creative minds. This is a win-win for all!

THE WHOLE FAMILY BENEFITS

Okay … I took the high road by first explaining the benefits of playgroup for the kids' best development. I have to confess here, though, I, as a mom, as a person, may have benefited the most. The friendships that developed between a few of those moms and me helped save my sanity on many occasions. We exchanged cooking recipes and gave each other tips on how we were handling teething or butt rashes. It became a whole-family benefit when the dads showed up. They started attending barbecues and hunting together, sometimes with the kids and sometimes without.

> **There is a special closeness when the whole family enjoys the company of another whole family.**

There is a special closeness when the whole family enjoys the company of another whole family. Halloween stands out in my mind because we would get together as families. The dads would have a beer while the moms tried to perfect last-minute costume details, and then maybe we'd have a cookout. Afterward we'd all go trick-or-treating. Of course, I have tons of photos of this time of our lives, but one stands out: it's a panoramic picture of all the kids dressed up in their Halloween costumes. Just thinking about it makes me smile with nostalgia.

Still to this day we have family reunions, and even though our lives went in different directions when the kids went to their various colleges, we still talk, laugh, and pick up right where we left off. In fact in just a few weeks, we're going to Cabo with four couples that we met through these playgroups.

Make the time to get together with other families and allow everyone to play. Develop those family friendships, and commit to them. Kids who have consistent playgroups, from at least age two to six, benefit the most from the experience. Why? Dealing with people in long-term friendships will always result in having to learn long-term communication skills, more patience, tolerance, understanding, empathy, and ability to deal with diverse personalities. All that comes from playgroup in a family's life.

My tip? Get involved with great people and either start or join playgroups with your kids.

Halloween playgroup.

THE IMPORTANCE OF HAVING FAMILY MEALS TOGETHER

Getting everyone together around the table for a meal is a critical family activity, and it's important to start during toddlerhood. Why?

Thefamilydinnerproject.org reports the following benefits to kids who have regular family meals—a "meal" being defined as breakfast, lunch, or dinner. Just take a look at these advantages:

- Better academic performance
- Lower risk of substance abuse
- Lower likelihood of eating disorders
- Bigger vocabulary in preschoolers
- Greater sense of resilience
- Lower risk of depression
- Higher self-esteem
- Lower risk of teen pregnancy
- Lower rates of obesity
- Better cardiovascular health in teens
- Healthier eating patterns in young adults

There are also benefits for adults:

- Better nutrition with more fruits and vegetables and less fast food
- Increased self-esteem
- Less dieting
- Lower risk of depression

Family meals should become one of their deepest memories, a time when the family focuses on one another and enjoys time together. Each family member should feel free to discuss his or her day and what is on his or her mind. Laugh often and bring the conversation down to the kids' level. Silence the phones and keep them in a drawer! Turn the TV off, and enjoy the meal.

Positive memories of family mealtime will stay with your children forever. In fact we made it a point to have breakfast, lunch, and dinner together. Great conversations evolved during those times. If dinner time shifted to a later hour just so we could all sit down at the table together for a meal, so be it.

My sons will still ask about dinner if they don't see preparations happening by six o'clock. If they won't be there because they're eating tacos with friends instead, they let me know. If I won't be able to cook for whatever reason, I let them know, and alternate plans are made. It's just assumed that a family dinner will take place, and I make sure it does. (My husband even said I turned out to be a pretty good cook!)

TABLE MANNERS: EVERYONE NOTICES

Did you know that childcare professionals can actually spot the toddlers who have family meals at home? Kids who regularly sit at a table that is set with eating utensils are the ones who know how to sit still at the preschool table and eat their birthday cake with a spoon or kids' fork; they know how to use utensils, napkins, etc. Although they may not be the most dexterous at using those items, the concepts are not foreign to them.

Kids without this experience are literally upside down in their chair, sometimes without the slightest idea of how to eat at a table— and others do notice.

The toddler years are the best years to teach table manners, especially by demonstration. If a child grows up with manners being displayed, it will be easy to pick up on. We had a rule in our house, for instance, that no one left the table before everyone else was done eating. Each person then rinsed his own plate and put it in the dishwasher. Well, toddlers can handle these rules, and with help they certainly can learn this simple courtesy.

Along with proper napkin and fork usage, the toddler stage is a particularly good time to teach social etiquette. Here are my best toddler-specific tips on social etiquette at the table:

Teach Them Conversation: This isn't about the child learning to talk as much as it's about learning to converse, follow a topic, and provide input. Of course, a toddler of one to four years of age will not follow complex topics, but they will learn conversation if you bring it down to their level: "What did you like about story time today? Was your teacher a good reader? If we go for ice cream after practice, what flavor would you like?"

When your child answers you, respond: "I like readers who do the voices too; I'll bet that was fun! You're getting chocolate ice cream again? I think I might try strawberry this time." Engage in conversation with your toddler.

Ask Specific Questions: I'm sure all of us have seen an adult try to speak to a child, and the child just stares silently back at the adult. We all likely know, as well, that as kids get older, the silence can turn into one-syllable grunts of some sort that in no way resemble conversation.

The way around this is never to ask an open-ended question: "What did you do today? How was lunch? What's new?"

Instead, ask specific questions: "When you were at preschool today, did you see your friend Easton? Were you able to play superheroes on the playground? What superhero were you?"

If you engage your child at their level, they become adults you can have real conversations with. For instance, I have a note right here to discuss Astros tickets with my sons at dinner. Yes, we can have a group text about it, but I enjoy talking to them. They grow to be enjoyable adults if you enjoy them during their childhood.

Make Family Mealtime Routine: Again, it doesn't matter if you regularly share breakfast, lunch, or dinner as a family. If a member of the household works nights, they might get home just in time to have breakfast with the family. Maybe mom or dad works evenings, and the lunch hour is when everyone is home. What is important is that you create as much routine around mealtime as possible, because routine creates security in the child and keeps the task on track.

QUICK, HEALTHY MEALS

My mother was "meal prepping" before it was ever a trendy term. She usually cooks all day on Sunday, and then she serves the meals throughout the week or freezes them for quick dinners down the road.

I plan for only a few days at a time, according to the calendar with everyone's events on it. Once I see what the schedule looks like, I make meal decisions and shop twice a week for supplies.

Regardless of how meals are planned, it's often critical in a busy household for healthy meals to be prepared, eaten, and cleaned up quickly. My household is nonstop, so I found that these tips work best for delicious, healthy meals that are ready fast:

Use a Crockpot: There are endless, delicious recipes you can make with a crockpot or Instant Pot. The beauty of this cooking method is that if schedules bring family members home at different times, the meal is hot and ready for them. This really is my go-to cooking method, especially during baseball season!

Use the Grill: Grilling chicken, chops, fish, burgers, steaks, etc., on the grill can produce the quickest meals, and they can easily and quickly be paired with healthy side dishes. Bonus: the cleanup is typically easy!

Use an Air Fryer: Last night I cooked salmon in thirteen minutes using my air fryer, and it was delicious. I'm finding this appliance to be outstanding for quick, healthy meals. I also love that I can improve the health quality of traditionally greasy, old-world foods by cooking them in the air fryer.

THE TODDLER ROUTINE AND BEDTIME

In the newborn stage, if you remember, I recommended feeding the infant last in your routine because the baby would be up again in three hours.

In the toddler stage, we still want to exhaust the child during the day with outside activities, playgroup visits, and movement, but now we eat dinner, have bath time, then have story time.

The classical music is on, curtains have been closed, you're rocking the child in the rocking chair. It won't take long until they are sound asleep.

RIDDING THEM OF THE PACIFIER

Ryan, my second son, was addicted to his pacifier—or "pe-te," as he referred to it. Just around the age of two, I decided enough was enough: it was time to lose the pe-te forever. As it happened we were building our forever home at that time, and we were living in a temporary apartment. In a few months, everything would be new: his bed, his room, his whole house. It would be too overwhelming for any child to take on that many stressors at the same time they're dealing with letting go of their pacifier.

I started by getting a clear plastic container, putting a handful of pacifiers in it, and tying it to his crib. Every week I'd remove one. The conversation would go something like this: "Last week you had five pacis, and now there are only four. Do you remember losing one?" Of course he didn't remember because he didn't lose it; I took it away. "Is it under the bed?" We looked, and there was no pacifier under the bed. "Hmm … I wonder where your pacis keep going."

This sequence was repeated until he was down to one pacifier. I let him hold onto that for about two more weeks, then just took it away. He never cried, never sucked his thumb; it just went away with this weaning process.

If you're ready to pass the pacifier right into the trash, I hope this method helps! Whatever you do, be sensitive to the child and how you approach this. They have an emotional attachment to the pacifier; it's how some kids comfort themselves. Be sure everyone is ready before taking it away.

CHORES? FOR A LITTLE TODDLER? YOU BET!

I knew I wanted kids, but I also knew I wasn't going to be the maid for a houseful of people. Hear me, moms and dads: I refused to be taken advantage of, so I put chores in action to keep that from happening.

I actively assigned chores, meaning I was aware and on top of the assignment. I didn't just create a rule, then they were on their own or we all forgot about it. I actively enforced it. I'm outright saying that this is the best parenting tip I can give you. This technique puts you in charge but more like an undercurrent that guides rather than a hurricane that's very loud but is ultimately the opposite of productive. Here are a few examples of what I'm talking about:

I had a rule that when we came in from outside, we had to remove our shoes and place them in their spot (colored bins for the child's shoes work great for this). Good rule, right? Toddlers will think this is fun, so get them into this habit now! Once it's routine, they just know, "This is how our house functions."

> **I actively assigned chores, meaning I was aware and on top of the assignment. I didn't just create a rule, then they were on their own or we all forgot about it. I actively enforced it.**

Now I didn't leave them to their own interpretation of what was expected. Number one, we led by example: we walked in the door, and Scott and I stopped and removed our shoes and jackets and put them away. It was expected and taught that the kids do likewise.

At the toddler stage, I suggest making this an adventure: "Let's make sure to hang our jackets. You're big enough to reach the hook, right?" (Make sure they can reach the hook!)

When they succeed, stay engaged by praising them. "Great job; I knew you were big enough."

Do you see what I mean? Using this method, I stayed actively engaged, but I did not touch the jacket or the shoes. They were, however, regularly put away in their proper places.

INCONVENIENCE THEM!

As toddlers grow and know better, the "fun" of doing tasks wears off. So, let's say the family arrives home from an exciting day, and the child is looking forward to a snack. They run in and drop their jacket on the floor en route to the kitchen. This is perfectly normal, but your goal is to have them picking up after themselves as a habit. To create the habit, they must remember to perform the task routinely.

First, of course, I see the jacket before it even hits the floor—typically, about six inches from its hook. Three scenarios come to mind on how this can be handled:

Scenario #1: I can pick the jacket up and put it on the hook for him. (Please don't do this, especially if you've already established the rule!)

Scenario #2: As soon as I see it falling, I can rush to remind him that it goes on the hook. This isn't a bad method of enforcing the rule, as long as the child is the one to complete the task.

Scenario #3: This option was my preferred way, and that was to make the task as inconvenient as possible for them, so they never forgot to do it again. I'd let them get all the way to the snack counter, then calmly proclaim, "Guess what? We are all ready for snack, but I noticed your jacket is on the floor. Where do we put our jackets? Go ahead and put it on the hook, and then we'll have snack."

Did the school-aged child leave his backpack sitting on the kitchen table? We'll discuss that when he's in the car, anxious to get to practice. Then he has to go all the way back and hang the book bag up, delaying his arrival at the field.

Friends stayed the night and didn't pick up their pillow and sleeping bag? That would be my respective son's responsibility because it was his friend who stayed over.

Do you see what I mean? I'm on top of everything, but they carry it through. Believe it or not, chores encourage involvement and provide a sense of accomplishment and responsibility. This is actually another way to bond with your toddler.

THE ATTENTION BAG

This tip saved me every time and always worked at restaurants, on planes, or even at doctors' offices. The "attention bag" is a bag filled with desirable toys that the child can play with—however, it's only given to them when they're in a situation where they need to sit still. The attention bag contains new or different toys than the ones the child typically plays with. When you pack your attention bag, think of the way your child's mind works. One mom, at least, reports being able to quiet her bundle of activity for nearly an hour just by giving him a few ten-piece puzzles from Dollar Tree.

I, personally, recall going on airplanes with four small boys, and when we entered the whole plane seemed to groan. They obviously assumed we were going to cause four straight hours of noise and distraction to our fellow travelers. By the time we deplaned, nearly every time, flight attendants and copassengers alike would compliment us on having such well-behaved kids … I always had the attention bag!

Here are some suggestions for some items you could add to an attention bag for toddlers:

- Cheerios
- Play-Doh
- Markers
- Crayons
- Stickers
- Paper
- Glue sticks
- A learning device

CELEBRATE YOUR CHILD'S BIRTHDAY!

I mentioned that I'm Hispanic, and my family is very close, so having big birthday celebrations was always an enjoyable tradition for me and my whole family. I've come across many parents these days who don't throw their kids birthday parties. I honestly don't mean to judge any mom, ever, who is really trying to do her best, but this really surprises me.

Celebrating your child's life adds a critical sense of value to his or her self-worth. They see that other kids are celebrated, and they are not. In their little minds, this can be highly devaluing. Especially if your family and friends have birthday traditions, try to stay in line with them. You can certainly still maintain individuality, but put the effort in, even if you aren't a creative type, to give your child a birthday celebration.

Now our style was to celebrate in a big way. You may be quieter, and your child—and budget—might have a better birthday celebration with a few close friends. Maybe your family tradition is to go out for a nice dinner, avoiding the kids' party altogether. How you celebrate isn't as important as making sure to pay special attention to the celebration.

START A FAMILY TRADITION

Starting a family tradition of your own is an amazing way to record your children's growth from year to year. I know some families, for instance, who open only one gift on Christmas Eve, but they share those gifts around the fireplace with close family. One family I know celebrates holidays the week prior to their actual date for logistical reasons.

In the toddler years, Scott and I began the family birthday tradition of taking a birthday candle to their bed and waking the birthday boy up by gently singing happy birthday. Everyone is still in pajamas and sleepy eyed, and the photos go from birthday to birthday through the years. They are some of my favorite memories.

During the toddler years, when the children are young and impressionable, begin a tradition that will last. Once they go off to college, the time for this type of memory will be gone. The tradition itself should be enjoyable and bring a sense of inclusion to the family members. Start your family tradition in the toddler years, and later in the book I'll show you how they come back to reward you.

TRUST YOUR INTUITION

To close out our toddler-stage section, I want to emphasize one final tip, and that is to trust your intuition.

When Dawson began sleeping in a twin bed, we put a safety gate on the bed to help him transition. Everyone was still getting used to this, and I kissed him good night one night and left, forgetting to lift the gate in place.

We were sound asleep, and we heard this bloodcurdling scream that sent us running down the hall. There was my three-year-old, on the floor. Relieved, we realized he'd simply fallen out of bed. Like we did with most mild injuries, we comforted him and reassured him that everything was all right.

We tried to put him back to bed, but Dawson was having none of it. He seemed to almost refuse to be comforted, and this wasn't like him. My husband felt sure that the sudden fall had only scared him, and we needed to put him safely back to bed and get some sleep ourselves.

I disagreed, but I didn't want to turn it into a fight in the middle of the night, so reluctantly I went back to bed.

I was guilt-ridden for having left that gate open; surely that was why I was so anxious. But …

Dawson didn't seem right …

No …

Something was wrong!

I slipped out of bed and went to Dawson's room again. He was in bed, but he was whimpering and favoring his side. I went to move his arm, and my baby screamed in agony. I was immediately on mom adrenaline. He needed to go to the hospital.

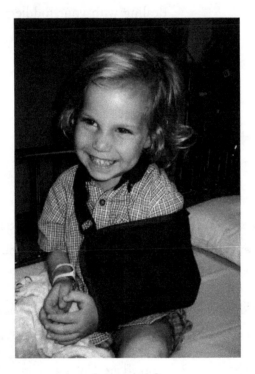

Dawson age 2.

I threw something on, picked him up, and I walked out the door with him, never even telling Scott what I was doing. When we got to the hospital, they x-rayed Dawson, and it turned out he had a broken collarbone. My guilt for leaving the gate down quadrupled, but I learned a valuable lesson that night. Scott's advice was usually very sound, and I knew he acted in the best interest of the kids. The more he said Dawson was fine, however, the more my intuition screamed that something was wrong. In the end my intuition was right—and yours will be too.

> **Listen to reason, but follow your intuition.**

Moms, you've been given intuition as a protection for your children, and it's something that even fathers don't fully understand sometimes. My final tip for dealing with your toddlers is to *listen to reason, but follow your intuition.*

• • •

JOURNALING IN THE TODDLER YEARS

CAPTURE IT!

Since one of the most-asked questions when it comes to journaling continues to revolve around what to write, I wanted to provide a few more examples from my own journals. Remember, what's important to you is important!

Avery would say this all the time: "Are you having a 'mojo' day?" His nickname was Duda.

Driving to school and Ryan asked me, "Where do trees and grass come from?" I answered, "From God; it is Mother Nature." Then Ryan asked me, "Where do children come from?" I answered, "From mommies and daddies." Ryan then said to me that when he was in my tummy, he didn't remember seeing anything but blood.

Eating dinner at the table, Ryan is aged four, and he says to me, "Mom, I am diggin' on your food!"

Ryan, age five, funny story: Ryan Boochini (nickname) says, "Look what I tied onto my penis!"

I turn and see a rubber yoyo looped around Ryan's penis. He moved it around by swaying back and forth, with a great big smile on his face. I explained to him how delicate his penis is and that he should never tie or put anything on it. Horrorstruck, he said to me, "I will never do that again." He was so upset because he placed his penis in danger.

Something always heard in our house when Avery was about six and Ryan was four. "I'm on a mission!" They would just giggle uncontrollably.

October 16, 2006: Reece is three years old—looks at me and says, "Mommy, you are precious!"

Reece's nicknames: Lu-Lu Malulu! (Slang word in Spanish for naughty), Reecaroni, "Little Gremlin."

Reece, age four, funny story: I was reading Reece a bedtime story and took my strapless bra off to be more comfortable. Reece holds the bra up and says, "Mommy, you took your boobies off!"

Dawson's nicknames: Baby D, Baby Dawson, Didi, and D-Raw.

As I said, I often grabbed a Post-it and captured the moment. My tip would be to adopt a similar way of recording memories, perhaps using your phone. The point is to capture it immediately because, even though you believe you will remember, we tend to forget the details.

CHAPTER 5

THE ELEMENTARY YEARS (AGES FIVE TO TEN)

You may notice that this chapter on the elementary years is longer than all the others. There is a practical reason for so much material in this one stage. It's because in these years you're building on the foundation we began in the previous stages. You really are trying to get as much "built" into them as possible during the elementary years.

This is when kids transition from babyhood to capable humans who can handle responsibility. They understand rules and consequences at this stage. They're malleable, they become capable of performing chores adeptly, and they can consistently carry through on them to a point of routine—which is what we want.

> **You really are trying to get as much "built" into them as possible during the elementary years.**

Continue asking specific questions when you communicate: "What are you learning in science? Did your teacher give any examples? My favorite science experiment was dissecting a frog ..."

Remember to be that steady undercurrent guiding them, rather than a storm in their lives during these critical years.

HONEST ... TO A FAULT

You may find your elementary-stage child to be mature enough to reason but too innocent to understand anything except total honesty. This can cause highly awkward situations, and I don't believe there really is a tip in the world that will prepare you for the embarrassment your pure-hearted child may cause with his or her candid remarks.

Scott had a head-on collision with elementary-stage honesty when he volunteered to read a story to Dawson's kindergarten class. He'd become a very engaging reader to our boys, so he was really looking forward to the experience. He took some time selecting just the right book, stepped confidently into the classroom, and slam!

This lovely, blond-haired little girl was squinting at him, like a question was forming that was about to bust out. He noticed her because she was sitting in the front row, dead center, about six feet in front of him. He condensed his body into the fourteen-inch-high chair that was provided, introduced himself as Dawson's dad, and explained that he was going to read one of Dawson's favorite books. Believing that he was perfectly clear, he began the story.

He didn't get through the first sentence when this little girl's hand shot up. She said, "Excuse me. Can I ask a question?"

Scott said, "Sure."

She responded, "Whose grandpa are you?"

Scott looked around, thinking someone else had walked in. Then he realized she was referring to him! Her dad was likely in his thirties, while Scott was in his fifties. He clearly looked more her grandpa's age than her dad's. A bit deflated, he pasted a smile on his face and explained that he was Dawson's daddy, not his grandpa.

Her honesty caught him completely off guard, and a bit self-consciously he finished the story, the whole time with this little girl's eyes nearly crinkled shut trying to figure out how this could be.

THEY'RE WATCHING *YOU*; BE A ROLE MODEL

Similar to the way that kindergartener tilted her head and watched Scott in fascination, your kids are watching everything you do, and oftentimes you will have to sacrifice to show them the right path. This concept cemented itself in Scott and me one day when Avery was in the elementary stage.

We have a large friend group, and the "red Solo cup" with an alcoholic drink in it was something all the dads—and some of the moms—regularly drank from. Not only was it a blatant symbol of "Hello, I'm drinking alcohol," but Avery, when he was eight years old, had accidentally taken a gulp from one of the red Solo cups. If it ever was a secret that booze was in those cups, the jig was up now. (Thankfully he said it tasted yucky!)

One evening we were at home, and Scott decided to have a gin and tonic. Of course, he had to put it in a red Solo cup, even though we do have all kinds of other options. At one point in the evening, Avery wanted to shoot hoops in the driveway, and Scott's car was blocking that spot. Like nothing, Scott walks outside, juggling his keys and the red Solo cup, which was still in his hand. He took a good sip of his drink before setting it on the porch step and getting in the car to move it. I almost flew to the car door, scaring him with my wild-eyed expression.

He was only going to reverse down our own driveway about ten feet, just to give Avery room to shoot, and he wasn't intoxicated by any means. As I stood there, I could tell he had no idea what the problem was. I said loudly, "You have been drinking; you can't get behind the wheel."

At first he didn't get it. "What do you mean? I'm not driving anywhere. I'm just backing down the driveway."

Then I locked eyes with him in that we-are-a-parental-unit way and said, "But you've been drinking, and we don't drink and drive, because it's dangerous." I nodded my head toward Avery, who was watching carefully. Scott finally realized the optics he was displaying. I ended up moving the car, and that incident stuck in Scott's mind. It was, perhaps, the first time he realized just how much influence his everyday actions had on our kids.

He began to intentionally role model the behavior he wanted them to emulate, especially when it came to drinking and driving. Looking back it's kind of funny how obvious he was, but throughout our kids' predriving years, he'd dramatically set his red Solo cup down and announce that he couldn't drive anywhere now because he'd had a drink. Meanwhile we were in for the night and had no intentions of going anywhere. As the boys got older and began driving themselves, Scott reinforced this thinking by directly asking one of them to drive if he'd had a drink.

Your kids will do what you do, not what you say. Kids of smokers often smoke; kids whose parents don't exercise tend not to prioritize exercise; and kids who are raised on a steady diet of chicken fingers and fries may continue to eat this way even if their health is at risk later in life.

It's important to assess, then, what you want them to do, and do it yourself by way of example. Successful role modeling will require sacrifice on the parents' parts.

LADIES AND GENTLEMEN ... UH, GENTLEMEN?

When we assessed what we wanted for our sons, a few qualities were prioritized: we wanted them to be healthy, so we cooked healthy meals with lots of vegetables; we wanted them to be well mannered, so we were sure to demonstrate good manners by saying please; thank you; yes, sir; and yes, ma'am to cashiers and elders alike; and we wanted them to have understanding and empathy for others, so we volunteered with them at different aid organizations, including the Houston Food Bank.

Another area I felt strongly about is the fact that I wasn't raising boys; I was raising men, who'd be married one day with families (hopefully). It was important to me that they understood good manners between ladies and gentlemen.

During these formative years, I began discussing how gentlemen protect girls' reputations by not discussing private things that would hurt them. I explained that gentlemen hold the door for a lady, pull out a chair for her at the dining table, and don't just talk about themselves, but they ask relevant questions about someone they are conversing with.

Then this bombshell hit me: Scott and I really weren't role modeling all those qualities. We loved each other completely, and we were best friends, but we'd been through life together, and I'm afraid the demonstrations of daddy holding doors and pulling out chairs were lacking. So, I pulled Scott aside and explained—a few times—that if they grow up seeing their mother treated like a lady and dad acting like a gentleman, they will do likewise. As their dad it was his job to role model this behavior. As their mom it was my job to accept these courtesies. (By far my favorite rule in the house!)

GIFTS FOR ME? WHY, THANK YOU!

Another way I took control of role modeling was in the area of gift giving. Moms, we'll talk quite a bit about getting out of your emotional brain and taking on a problem-solving mindset. If you have a husband, like mine, who's extremely busy and just not a great gift giver, this one is for you!

Scott honestly did try in our earlier years to be on top of the gift-giving occasions. Unfortunately, this is just not a strength for him. My confident, social husband just about locks up over what to buy. I spent some time being hurt and bewildered by this, but then I thought of the boys. I wanted them to understand the value of a mother/female in the home, not only for me but for their future wives. I felt that recognizing gift-giving occasions, especially birthdays, demonstrated that value.

So I began buying myself the things I wanted, wrapping them, and gifting them to myself, from Scott, at my birthday celebrations. I'd tell him, "I really needed some new sneakers, so I bought myself a pair for my birthday next month. They are wrapped and in your closet."

When he "gave me" the gift, he'd say it was from him and all the boys. This demonstrated that gifts for their mom—and down the road, for their wives—are special and something to pay attention to. Eventually I bought one for each of them, so on my birthday I had five gifts to open (bonus)!

Because I love birthdays, mine lasts a week, not a day. The best part about that is the boys get to see me wearing their gift. If they gave me those sneakers, they see me wearing them. If they gave me a little heart necklace, they see I'm wearing the necklace; it's not forgotten in the closet. This is a win-win-win: the boys are learning; I am getting what I want (without having hurt feelings or starting fights); and Scott is relieved of gift-buying duty.

Along similar lines, whenever we were invited to someone's home for dinner, I was sure to point out that we brought a gift to the host family. Just as I had hoped, it made them ask why we brought a gift if it wasn't anyone's birthday. This gave me the chance to explain a critical piece of social etiquette: when someone invites you to their home, it's right to thank them with a gift. It might be a bottle of wine, a box of chocolates, one flower, or a bouquet. We taught them that the point is to honor your host for honoring you with an invitation.

Just a month or so ago, Ryan was invited to stay at a good friend's family home for Oklahoma University (OU) weekend. Out of the blue, he called me: "Mom, I need some ideas for what to give Grant's mom." He wanted to thank her for the invitation with a gift. Trust me, it does come around full circle.

UNPRODUCTIVE VERSUS PRODUCTIVE COMPLIMENTS

While you want to always provide positive reinforcement to your children, at the elementary stage, be cautious of tossing out unproductive compliments. Unproductive compliments are those that give some sort of status or credit for nonaction, basically for nothing or for unproductive things. I observed a situation where a young volunteer gushed over one child, repeatedly telling him, "You're so cute; you're just so cute!" This tiny three-year-old—with long blond hair, backward cap, and little-surfer swag, who was in fact adorable—was developing a not-so-adorable ego.

A better way to positively reinforce self-esteem is to train yourself to speak to your child by encouraging good character and skills. For example, "I love how you figured that out," or "You helped Ada put the dishes away? Great job; that was being very helpful."

As parents, make it a priority to speak to your elementary-stage child in a way that prioritizes honesty, integrity, respect, kindness, and problem-solving and organizational skills. These priorities will truly put your child on a path of success.

SCHEDULES DURING THE ELEMENTARY STAGE

It may feel like the schedules of elementary-age children take you on a dizzying journey, but the schedule during these years is really something you build. If you look at one twenty-four-hour day by blocks of time, there are four blocks: morning, afternoon, evening, and nighttime. Mornings are for getting ready for school, where they will be for about seven hours. At nighttime they are sleeping. This leaves afternoon (after school) and evening hours to fill. Be reasonable and effective in filling both blocks of time.

In our home, schoolwork took a major priority, so after-school time was dedicated to getting homework done. Our next highest priority was sports, and that took up our evenings, usually from about 5:30 to 8:00 p.m. Simple, right?

We all know it's not simple. Things like television and video games isolate school-age children's attention, and the next thing you know, they're staring at those things and ignoring your schedule completely.

What we did to counter this was to make a rule in our home that neither TV nor video games were allowed throughout the week,

Monday through Thursday. This, unfortunately, was a rule I had to adhere to as well. Why was this necessary? Because even if I had a talk show on—something not at all kid friendly—they were glued to the irresistible force of the television. Since I was the role model, there I was denying the whole house TV time in order to stay on track. (Role modeling will require sacrifice sometimes!)

From Friday through Sunday, they could watch as much TV and play as many video games as they wanted—almost. While this worked to some extent, what do you think they did from Friday to Sunday, nonstop? Video games. It was like we were starving them, and they had to fill themselves with as much game time as possible before the life supply was cut off again. Scott and I observed this with a bit of confusion. Our rule didn't seem to be working out as we expected it to, so we modified it, which is a parent's prerogative!

Our rule didn't seem to be working out as we expected it to, so we modified it, which is a parent's prerogative!

Scott came up with this qualifier: each week the boys had to select a book to read. Throughout the week they earned one minute of game time for every page of the book they would read. Suddenly, there was motivation to read so they could earn as much game time as possible.

My tip, if you try this method, is to be aware of what it will take for you to keep track of things—especially if you have more than one child. Use a simple method to track pages, like, "page-number start" and "page-number ending" for each reading session. You will need not only to track the number of pages read, but also to be at least somewhat aware of the book's theme, so you can verify what they've read and ask questions about their chosen book.

LIFE THROWS YOU CURVEBALLS— LOTS OF THEM!

You can do all the right role modeling and scheduling and keep them busy and have productive conversations, and still life itself seems destined to test you. We all want to believe our kids are perfect, but when life throws you curveballs, likely as not their struggles are what are hitting you in the face. As a parent, you will feel everything they go through in your heart. There's no such thing, really, as "they" have a problem.

My tip for life's curveballs is never to ignore a legitimate issue, but face it head on with a goal toward finding solutions. This isn't only sensible—to find solutions and take a support role in your child's struggle—it's your way to survive the heartache.

"Struggles" will come in all shapes and sizes, but there are those that make you focus—wide-eyed and scared—until the issue is resolved. In my home these were any type of physical or emotional struggle. Here are two examples that stand out:

PHYSICAL STRUGGLES: MY CHILD HAS *WHAT?*

Of all the things you will worry about in your parenting career, nothing will grip you more than if your child has a health challenge. Any type of physical limitation can launch your emotions into turmoil. My tip stands: pull yourself into problem-solving mode.

When Reece was about four, I started noticing that he had a voracious appetite. He could eat as much as I could, a full-grown adult.

These large meals were followed by harsh bowel movements, and thirty minutes later he would be telling me how hungry he was again.

I might not have worried if I'd seen him growing because of this. I mean growth spurts can happen at any age, and they are marked by unusual amounts of food intake. However, Reece wasn't growing; he seemed to be stunted in place.

When I realized this, I immediately brought my concerns up to his pediatrician. He "reassured" me that this was indeed a growth spurt—a growth spurt that went on for a year without growth!

Moms, remember what we discussed about your intuition? Don't let anyone tell you something that goes against it. When something told me to inspect the toilet after one of my son's visits, I noticed his poop would float. I thought this unusual enough to bring it up to his doctor, who again brushed me off.

Fourteen months later Reece was due for his annual checkup, and finally the doctor looked at him and took us seriously. My son was behind on every single growth chart. With some sense of urgency now, his doctor referred us to an endocrinologist. Just the word alone, "endocrinologist," sent panic radiating through me. To my thinking, only very ill people needed such specialists.

The main symptoms Reece presented with at the endocrinologist's office were stunted growth, distended belly, and poor eyesight. The endocrinologist did all kinds of bloodwork, and decided, almost as an afterthought, to run a celiac panel. It was just a precaution; she seemed genuinely unconvinced that this panel would return positive.

Two days later in the car on the way to soccer, I got the call: Reece was positive for celiac disease. The symptoms he was having were alarming, so I braced myself for the worst. "What does this mean?" I asked, into my Bluetooth earpiece, trying to manage the conversation and the vehicle at the same time.

I was braced for the struggle of a lifetime, when the doctor casually responded with this: "He just has to eat 'gluten-free.'" I'm thinking, gluten ... okay ... gluten? What the heck is gluten?

The doctor continued, "Go over to Whole Foods, and you will find a selection." Just as the words came out of her mouth, I happened to be passing a Whole Foods. Surely this was a sign that all would be well.

We need to go back in time a bit here because "gluten-free" was a brand-new term in 2008, when we went through this. Jennifer Aniston, thankfully, began gluten-free awareness around the same time, in the mid-2000s. Back then they touted it as a method for weight loss, and today you can find products and even restaurants committed to the gluten-free lifestyle. At that time, however, no one even knew what gluten was. Where did it come from? How do I keep my child free of it?

You can imagine the effort it took to pull my emotions back in check. A diet was needed immediately to help my child, and I didn't even understand this enemy ingredient. Problem-solving had to kick in, so the first thing I did was learn about this condition. Scott went into action, printing ten pages off the internet to help us learn about celiac disease and how to eat gluten-free.

We learned that celiac is an autoimmune disease that does not allow the stomach villi to absorb nutrients. With proper diet, however, celiacs can lead completely normal, productive lives. This prompted a trip to Whole Foods, where I spent $300 on products that we literally threw away because they tasted so bad.

MY CHILD IS DIFFERENT

In the midst of this bomb going off in my household, it was time for school to start up again. When the elementary years begin, one of the first things your child will be subjected to is comparisons. The pecking order had begun, and because of the celiac condition, my Reece could see and feel his differences.

My tip for this type of soul-destroying dilemma is to take the lead as much as possible to balance things out for your child. My way was to become room mother and get involved in the parties and events he was a part of. As room mother I knew what treats were on our event menus. So, if Johnny's mom was bringing ice-cream cake for Johnny's birthday, I knew about it ahead of time, and I'd be sure to have a piece of gluten-free cake for Reece. If Chick-fil-A was being served at an event, I'd know, and I'd be sure to bring his gluten-free chicken nuggets on a heating pad so they were ready when the Chick-fil-A was served. I won't lie; it took a lot of preplanning, but I was more than happy to do whatever it took to even the odds for him.

Reece age 5, in glasses, beginning his celiac journey.

Even while I tried the best I could to be sure my son had what he needed to be included, he knew he was different. He'd ask me, "Why does everyone else get to eat superhero cake, and I can't? Why am I the only kid in class that has to wear glasses?" When he asked why his brothers didn't have celiac, we explained the science behind it, but we also reminded him that one of his brothers was asthmatic and Scott was on thyroid medication. We tried to make him see that he wasn't alone and that many people have differences.

Determinedly I searched for better answers, and if ever problem-solving and desperation paid off, it was at this juncture. I found a group called ROCK: Raising Our Celiac Kids, and I got very involved in the group. Finally I had a solid grasp on exactly what the problem was with gluten.

"Gluten is a protein found in many grains, including wheat, barley, and rye. It's common in foods such as bread, pasta, pizza, and cereal. Gluten provides no essential nutrients. People with celiac disease have an immune reaction that is triggered by eating gluten."[9]

I learned how to avoid it while still cooking delicious meals. I ran meetings and participated in recipe swaps, which helped immensely. In a nutshell I got involved in ROCK so my son could see that other kids had the same challenges. This worked on two major levels: the delicious foods, absent the problem ingredient, caused him to grow and catch up with his peers; and the new friend group made him feel normal.

You will feel everything they feel, and my tip is to turn it around. Focus the child's attention on the many great things they have. I set out to constantly remind all my boys how important family was, and we were sure to make Reece always feel loved and accepted in our

---

9   Robert H. Shmerling, "Ditch the Gluten, Improve Your Health?" April 14, 2022, Harvard Health Publishing, https://www.health.harvard.edu/staying-healthy/ditch-the-gluten-improve-your-health.

family. We created mottos like, "We're a unit," and we made sure that the struggling member of the unit understood his unmatched value.

Our poor-sighted little boy with the distended belly is now five feet nine inches tall, with twenty-twenty vision, and he knows how to cook and what to eat to avoid dietary issues. *Concentrate on solutions when life throws you curveballs.*

Reece age 18.

EMOTIONAL STRUGGLE: HIGH ANXIETY EVERY SINGLE DAY

Almost as frightening as physical/health concerns are any type of emotional struggle in your child. In the elementary stage, the "unaware baby" is changing, and a more emotionally aware individual is emerging. While that's normal, it can be an overload for some kids. Avery had such a reaction.

During his kindergarten year, he started having anxiety completely out of the blue. My baby was panicking and clinging to me when he had to go to school, and I had to send him into this situation every single weekday. It was heartbreaking, and it was affecting him socially at school.

My tip for these types of struggles stands: find solutions. Get out of your emotional brain and get into problem-solving mode. I didn't say it was easy; I'm saying it's necessary for your child. If they see you approaching emotional upset with an effort at making things better, they will associate the emotional upheaval as something to overcome. If you ignore it or, worse, coddle it, baby them, or allow their emotions to rule you and your home, they will learn that unhealthy emotional episodes are uncontrollable, and it gets them what they want. I did not want that, so this is what I did:

Gather Information: First off, I spoke to the teacher to be sure he wasn't being bullied in some way. I was the room mother, mind you, and I knew his teacher very well. We both agreed we saw no signs of harassment and no outward circumstances that would legitimately cause this anxiety. Thankfully we checked that off our list.

Keep It Upbeat, and Prepare Them for Weaning: I've been using the strategy of preparing my children for change from the time of infancy. If you remember, I used this to wean them from the pacifier and also to potty train. For this new challenge, I went the same route: I started by telling him fun stories on the drive to school or reminding him of great memories, like our family vacation to Disney, and keeping the air light. I never mentioned anything school related, because that would bring on the anxiety.

Engage the Weaning Process: I gradually weaned him from his separation anxiety by first parking the car and walking him to his class, all the while keeping his mind on fun things. Every day I added something to the conversation, like this: "Hey, it's the month of September. In the month of October, I can't walk you in anymore. I can only drop you off at the curb in October, so the flag-patrol person will walk you up to the door." We had observed the flag-patrol person walking other kids in, and we'd say, "Hello," so this wasn't foreign.

It was an emotionally trying time, but the mental preparation worked. He went with the flag-patrol person at the beginning of October, and he was soon bounding out of the car with barely a wave goodbye.

• • •

My final tip on emotional struggles is to never let your child feel alone, especially during emotional episodes. Work through it with your child with a goal toward seeing them grow past the issue.

It may take some time, so shore up your strength, and prepare them through.

KEEPING THEM CLOSE

You may begin to feel your child drifting away from you or getting very independent at some point in the elementary stage. This is actually very normal, but there are things you can do, attitudes you can take on, to keep your maturing little ones close. Here are three strategies we developed through the years to maximize our time with our boys and keep the lines of communication open:

> **We let the boys know early on that our house is a "safe house."**

Safe House: Probably the most important thing is that we let the boys know early on that our house is a "safe house." They can talk to us, as their parents, about anything or anybody—brothers, uncles, teachers, friends—and it will be respected as confidential. We literally say, straight out, "This is a safe house. What is said in confidence will not leave these four walls."

Weekly Talks: We made a habit of pulling each one of our boys aside separately each week just to talk to them. For us it was Sunday afternoon, and we make this appointment the same each week to ensure it's scheduled in. This isn't the time to discipline or scold the child; this is the time to let them talk about what's important to them. We chatted about friends, school, girls, if they'd been offered drugs, what was going on with their grades, and about anything that they may not want to say in front of their siblings.

Meal Dates: We had regular breakfast, lunch, or dinner dates with them. This means the parents and child leave the other kids at home and go out for the meal of their choice. I believe you will find this tip to be the most enjoyable. Not only do you relax when you're out and someone else is worrying about the meal, but the child feels grown up, special, and particularly apt to open up to you.

Moms, this is your chance to teach them to put their napkin in their lap, which glass is their water glass, how to identify the proper fork, and good manners in general. Dads, this is your time to discuss things from that all-important father's-eye view.

SPORTS AND KEEPING THEM *VERY* BUSY

Credit for this next tip really must go to Scott, but I had to implement it for years, so I'm convinced this is truth: sports are important in a child's life, especially for boys. Now I don't come from a very sporty, athletic family. I exercised, but I was never in softball or basketball, and my brothers limited themselves to soccer. I did have a try at ballet once; what a disaster that was. So this is something I saw in action and learned was good.

Scott was emphatic that sports molded good habits into children and kept them active and physically fit. He willingly stepped in to assist in this process by coaching almost every team our sons were on, and I was by his side as the "team mom." (Premoms, choose a man who will be a great dad!)

For those who think this view is a bit narrowminded, let's be very real here: we all want to look our best and feel our best. We all want to be able to speak intelligently in social gatherings. We all need to know how to lose ten pounds when necessary. Sports provides all this for a developing child.

Moms of boys, especially: those sweet little guys will be adults one day at their workplace. Inevitably the subject of "last night's game" will arise. Straight up they need to know how the main games work. They need firsthand knowledge of baseball, soccer, basketball, and football. As a man, your precious boy will be humiliated if he doesn't at least know the name of the game, what the love of the game is all about, and the difference between a point, a down, and a goal. This doesn't mean boys have to be in football, or any other sport, every year of their youth, but they need to be on a couple of teams to know how to understand, watch, and play the main four games. They need to know how to throw a spiral, because they will be laughed at if they don't know how to do that.

A young adult's self-esteem is largely wrapped up in how their physical appearance presents, and that's just a cold, hard fact. I strongly believe in giving kids the very best chance at that lifetime of confidence and good health by enrolling them in as many organized sports as possible. The "push" it takes to physically perform at any sport will eventually be the same push they reach for as an adult to get that bonus or that promotion. Boys build their self-esteem from being strong and athletic. Men build their self-esteem from being successful in their careers.

What about music, reading, and other worthwhile activities? Yes, yes, and yes! A pet phrase of Scott's is "Your favorite sport needs to be math because later on it will be math that takes you where you want to go." Keep them engaged in all the things that interest them, in addition to sports and regular physical activity.

It takes commitment on the parents' part to learn when sign-ups are, communicate with coaches and other parents, get them to the right field on the right day and at the right time, sit through all the games, bring snacks, make sure uniforms are purchased and cleaned in time for each game, etc., etc., but I wholeheartedly believe this is one of the best strategies to move kids into adulthood: keep them very busy!

PLAYDATES IN THE ELEMENTARY STAGE

You might see playdates as a practice that should start dying out when the school years begin. After all, everyone is so busy, and they see their friends every day at school. Emphatically I encourage you to rethink that!

During the elementary years, you still have control of playdates, and having friends over is a great way to get them off the gaming console. We used to make the arrangements and not even tell the boys. A knock at the door would sound on a day off school, and there would be a friend for each of them.

Here's the tip: don't send them off with their friends to simply figure out what to do, because they will likely do what? Play video games. No. Plan activities for playdates. We would take them swimming, go bike riding, play board games, bake cookies, anything to keep them away from TV and gaming.

CHORES DURING THE ELEMENTARY STAGE

Children who are between five and ten years of age are absolutely capable of doing chores. Admittedly the five- to seven-year-old may have to start with simplified versions of chores, but sometimes we as parents continue to see our "baby" as just that—a baby who isn't able to perform tasks. Please don't look at your child in that way. Take note of their growth and capabilities and allow them to help. A child in the elementary stage, and especially in the eight-to-ten-year-old range, is perfectly capable of performing the following tasks and more.

Washing Clothes: When my older three boys were in the elementary stage, I employed a housekeeper who would come once per week. This can cause a certain laziness to develop in kids or a lack of ability to "see" what they do to their own environment. I was not having that. The housekeeper worked for me. The children still had to learn the tasks needed to keep house. With this in mind, I started having them bring all their dirty clothes to the laundry room the day the housekeeper was due to arrive, and it was their job to sort them.

If you recall, in the previous stages we taught by demonstrating the chore consistently: "We all put our coats on the hook and our shoes in their place." This is still the process; however, in the elementary stage we are handing the chore off to them. What do I mean?

Very simply, when you teach them, be sure to allow them to actually do the job. When the boys started sorting laundry, it was necessary to teach them how to sort light colors from darks or white laundry. After the lessons they earned credit for handling this chore correctly without my constant supervision. We were not big on money rewards and instead would go for ice cream, special dinner places, or to a movie.

During summer, because there was more time, the added responsibility of washing the clothes was required. Yes, my seven- and eight-year-olds were taught, specifically, how to measure detergent, how to determine if the load should be washed in hot, warm, or cold water, and to listen for the dryer or set their own timers in order to remove the clothes before wrinkles overtook them.

My tip for assigning a chore, especially in the elementary stage, is to take time with each child to teach them the task. If they don't immediately pick up on the process, be patient.

Fixing Their Bed/Straightening Their Room: One of the easiest jobs to start with when it comes to chores is teaching them to fix their bed. I know this seems simple, but again, don't assume they know anything. I had to instruct them to pull the sheets all the way up, nice and tight, then the comforter, then place the pillows on top (no random tossing of the pillows). Straightening their room should also be an easy concept: Toys go in their box/place, and trash goes in the trash can.

One tip for bed fixing is, if your elementary-stage child has difficulty getting the covers straight, get on one side of the bed while they remain on the other side, and demonstrate the proper method.

Washing Cars: Washing cars is another chore that this age group loves to do, and you may be surprised at how good they are at it. Let them help you apply the suds and rinse the vehicle. Give them the "fun" task of collecting any garbage and/or vacuuming the interior. If they don't start out as pros, let those little muscles become accustomed to the task, and you'll soon see a skilled detailer.

Cleaning Toilets: Yes, 100 percent, your eight-to-ten-year-old is capable of cleaning toilets and doing a thorough job.

When we moved into our current home, the boys had their own bathrooms. Once again my attitude was that I was not cleaning the gallons of piss that flowed through those bathrooms! So I taught them, individually, the proper way to clean the toilet. As long as I kept all the supplies they needed easily accessible, they kept up on the cleaning and disinfecting of their own bathrooms (maybe with a bit of reminding).

Cooking and Baking: The elementary years were also when I started teaching my kids how to cook. We started with measuring, adding ingredients, and safely using the blender for baked goods. I gradually showed them some general kitchen concepts, like how to boil water, cook pasta, scramble or fry an egg, and make their own simple snacks. Safety was a big part of our discussions, so I stressed things like remembering to turn off the stove, never touching the spinning blades on the mixer or blender, and only using knives with proper supervision. (Dawson now makes better eggs than I do.)

Remove Trash/Recycling: Again this is an easy task that's very helpful to the household. For some unfathomable reason, the need to change the liner never occurs at a convenient time, so it often gets avoided until the trash legitimately forms a mountain.

My tip: if there's a helper who removes it for you, let them know how much of a help that is.

Dish Duty: Well before the age of ten, chores can graduate to things like emptying, loading, and unloading the dishwasher. Teach them how to properly clean plates and complete the task by fully drying the sink.

My tip on this is not to assume they know anything. I must have loaded the dishwasher thousands of times by the time they took on the task; you'd think they'd have observed the basics. Turns out, nope! The first time Avery loaded the dishwasher, I walked away, thinking my instructions were clear—a mistake. When I opened it after the cycle had finished, all the plates were lying flat on top of the dishwasher rack. All those years, and they didn't know to fit the plates in between the spokes of the rack.

• • •

So let's recap. By the age of ten, kids are easily capable of handling these areas of self-maintenance: they can prepare a snack, clean the mess completely, wash their own clothes, fix their bed, straighten their room, clean a bathroom, and perform general household chores that assist in the running of the household. If you feel these are attributes you'd like your child well trained in, teach them now! The goal is to teach them to handle themselves and their responsibilities without being reminded over and over.

If you start them off doing chores through these malleable years, you'll see them carry through with good habits when they're older.

One tip to help them, rather than constantly "tell" them, is to write Post-it note reminders, and put them in one obvious spot. For instance, smack dab on my sons' bathroom mirrors, there might have been notes saying, "Brush your teeth" or "You have a dentist appointment at three o'clock on Tuesday" or "Your book report is due Friday."

I've now seen two of my sons go through college, and while some freshmen didn't even know how to use a washing machine, my sons were able to easily do their laundry, tidy their dorm rooms, and clean their bathrooms—and they did it consistently! As I've been saying, if you start them off doing chores through these malleable years, you'll see them carry through with good habits when they're older.

THE SEX TALK IN THE ELEMENTARY STAGE

Children in the elementary stage are becoming aware of themselves and others, and this includes the sex organs. This can be a difficult topic for some parents to address. If you have any inhibitions about talking to your kids about sex, now is the time to get past it, because questions about sexuality are part of their awareness. I didn't sugarcoat things. We called boobs "boobs," vaginas were called "vaginas," and a penis was called a "penis."

This openness, I believe, stems from my upbringing. When I was a child, my parents were very out and open with just about everything. I remember being nine years old and waking up on a Sunday morning and wanting to go to my parents' bedroom to see if they were awake. There was usually a sign on the door that said, "Do Not Disturb."

Perhaps the best piece of advice I can give you for this arena is to be real with your kids because they will ask about body parts in the most curious way. When Avery and Ryan were about four and six, they were in the bathtub when I heard them having a very serious conversation. When I looked into the bathroom, my oldest had a ruler—an actual twelve-inch, plastic, school ruler, in the tub—and he and his brother were measuring their penises! I had to hide my laughter that time. After all, the discussion was pretty intense.

Be ready, be real, and be prepared to chuckle!

WHEN TO SAY WHAT

I recall talking about sex with Avery when he was in the middle school stage. Each child afterward, though, became more aware at younger and younger ages. Today, with iPads, iPhones, and the internet, clear discussions about sex need to take place at this younger elementary stage.

My husband started repeating this quote whenever he could get it into the conversation: "There are two things that will ruin your life: getting addicted to any type of substance or getting a girl pregnant." We were very open about why that is. Many a life has been cut short by drug addiction or sudden parenthood, and we spoke plainly about such consequences. Drugs rob people of their vitality, motivation, and intelligence. Pregnancy brings another life into the world—and that certainly cannot be ignored.

For all four of my boys, to answer questions and present a healthy analysis of sex, we used the book *Where Did I Come From? An Illustrated Children's Book on Human Sexuality* by Peter Mayle and Arthur Robins.[10] This book uses cartoon characters to illustrate the different aspects of puberty, what's happening in the girl's body, what's happening in the boy's body; then it goes into actual sexual intercourse and how a baby is made. It does get graphic, but it remains educational.

I also wasn't afraid to show them pictures of herpes infections and other venereal diseases. As intended these pictures grossed them out during the elementary years. In some cases the organs were unrecognizable, and I was certain to point out that this distortion of the sex organs happened when people had sex without wearing condoms. Then I explained that condoms could protect them from VD and pregnancy, so I stressed to always wear one.

---

10   Peter Mayle and Arthur Robins, *Where Did I Come From? An Illustrated Children's Book on Human Sexuality* (New York: Lyle Stuart, Inc., 1973).

MASTURBATION

I realize this one might be tough, but in this age group, kids may very likely become sexually aware of their own body, and they will naturally endeavor to relieve the tension of the situation.

One family I know had a ten-year-old who discovered his own erections and would "play with himself" wherever he was in the house. It was common for other family members to stroll into the living room, for instance, and there the child would be, going at it on the living room sofa.

When this mom came to me, a bit perplexed as to how to address this, my suggestion was to gently tell him that this is completely normal, but it's a private thing that should be done in his bedroom.

My tip: never scold them for their sexuality. However, it's okay to steer them onto acceptable social paths regarding it.

I did not restrict my sons from dating as they got older or try to curb their interest in sex. As a mother I honestly felt that if I didn't teach them proper respect for sex, they would learn lewd habits from the internet and friends.

My final tip for the sex talk during the elementary stage is to approach the subject with the attitude that the sex drive is perfectly normal, and they are growing normally, so be the one that they feel comfortable going to with their thoughts and questions.

WATCH WHO'S WATCHING YOUR CHILDREN

Let me preface this section by saying that twenty-five years ago there really wasn't a good vetting system for nannies and sitters. Today, there are agencies that automatically do background checks on their applicants, and you can find great people to help with childcare. Back then if you wanted a quality individual, you usually looked to the church, interviewed their respective applicant, and hoped it worked out. So that's exactly what I did.

I felt strongly that I didn't want someone else raising my kids, but Scott really felt that a nanny would be helpful. I guess I did need some help, because I went along with this idea, but I found I did not want someone in my way—I mean in my house—24-7. It's my house, you know what I mean? I know you do. Because I felt this way, I may have guarded my kids a bit during our short time of seeking a nanny, but honestly I'm glad I was vigilant.

With one, small items started going missing: my scissors one day, a hairbrush another, a pink pen, a tape recorder, and Dawson's favorite blanket (his NiNi), which he couldn't sleep without, all disappeared.

Now I never went through the housekeepers' personal items, but I started getting that feeling. After carefully thinking about it, one day when she was off, I went searching inside her room. Every missing item from the house was there. She went so far as to steal my maternity underwear! Who does that? Our nanny was a very weird kind of kleptomaniac! She was fired immediately.

Another nanny put my kids in the car while I went to the restroom—not a task that should require much guidance. On a one-hundred-degree day in Houston, Texas, where the humidity is so thick it can be difficult to breathe, she locked them in the car without opening any windows or turning on the air. When I sped out there and opened the door, it was steaming, and the kids were screaming, soaked with sweat. I was livid, and I don't regret my temper when I loudly fired her and threw her out of my house.

On top of everything, the incident caused me to miss an important baseball game for Avery. He was playing against his best friend, Adam's, team, and he hit a homerun. Missing that moment made me even angrier.

Yet another nanny regularly used my computer without my knowledge. How did I find this out? I had a virus on my computer that was causing it to act erratically. Derek, our tech guy, came over to check it out. He logged in ... then asked me in a careful, confused tone, "Jennifer, do you watch porn?"

"What? No! Why?"

He started pointing out all these images on my computer. Without detailing what I saw, I felt I knew who'd be interested in these scenes. I was in a state of shock when I finally spoke, "Oh my God, my nanny has been watching porn on my computer."

When I confronted her, she turned red and splotchy, obviously guilty. She too was fired immediately.

My point is to warn you to be very careful about who watches your kids. You really don't know a person who claims to be a childcare worker. Be selective. Not every nanny went so far as to steal or infect my computer with porn. One was simply more interested in watching TV. When I saw her impatiently ignore Avery because he wanted her attention during a program, I knew her style of childcare wasn't for me. You are absolutely within your right as a mom to insist on childcare that supports your values and meets your standards.

My tip: use a Ring camera, connected to your phone, as a safety net. We have a couple in our home. This way we as parents can always check in to see what's going on.

SUMMER HOMEWORK

Okay ... I did receive some criticism for my stance on this. Moms would ask me why I assigned schoolwork over the summer. My response was typically to ask what the kids would be doing otherwise. The answer was always the same: they'd be playing video games.

I can't stress enough times that TV and video overindulgence is unhealthy for elementary-age children. So I would start summer vacation by presenting each child with a blank journal. Learning to write the date and keep track throughout the summer was a requirement. They had to read me what they wrote, and I'd correct any spelling or punctuation issues. I would also give them a daily math sheet with questions appropriate to their math level.

The last "schoolwork requirement" was to pick a book to read for the summer. Most days we would have some sport or activity, such as a trip to the museum, and afterward I allowed them free time for electronics, but before any of that, reading was going to happen in our home.

My tip: keep book baskets all throughout the house!

SUMMER FUN!

No, we absolutely did not spend our summers exclusively doing homework! There is a lot of fun to be had! Informal activities like swimming and free play with toys should be regularly allowed. In addition, formal activities, those you plan for and "set out" to do, should be scheduled on a regular basis.

The elementary stage is the perfect time to take the children berry picking, horseback riding, to the museum, to the zoo, and to the beach. I recall several strawberry-picking trips where we brought home so many strawberries that we were giving them to neighbors, seeking out recipes, and baking as many strawberry-themed dishes as we could—yet another bonding experience.

Formal activities can also be done at home, with friends there to share it or just the family. A formal home activity is planned, and you

THE ELEMENTARY YEARS (AGES FIVE TO TEN)

as the parent are involved in its execution. Here are five of my favorite formal home activities:

Egg-Frying Experiment: As I mentioned, we live in Houston, where the temperatures go well into the hundreds. The teacher in me took this as a learning opportunity, and we would occasionally monitor the temperature outside by literally cracking an egg on the cement to see how long it took to fry.

My tip for those of you who live in cold-weather climates is to reverse this experiment by monitoring the winter temperatures. Set a few different size bowls of water outside to see how long it takes the different water depths to freeze.

Butterfly Cocoons: Amazon, Etsy, and a few other sites sell butterfly cocoons, and this can be both fun and educational for everyone. We would place them in a safe location and observe the process of butterflies emerging. It was an amazing experience each time we did it.

My tip would be to have a couple of facts to teach them about what's going on, and just enjoy this amazing act of nature with them.

Shaving-Cream and/or Water-Balloon Fights: These are fairly self-explanatory, but my first tip is put the kids in bathing suits!

For shaving-cream fights, give each child a can of shaving cream and a pair of goggles (to protect their eyes), then let them loose, spraying themselves and one another until they are ready to be hosed down. Kids and parents alike tend to have a blast throughout this activity. If you're feeling playful, grab a can for yourself, and take that party up a notch.

Water-balloon fights were along the same lines. I would fill hundreds of water balloons and let the boys go nuts in the backyard.

My tip is for pool owners: the shaving cream and/or balloons can ruin your pool mechanisms. Be sure to hose everyone down before allowing them in the pool, and keep broken balloon pieces far from the pool filter.

Raw Egg Toss: Begin by standing an equal distance apart from your teammate. One person begins by tossing the egg. If the teammate catches the egg, they both take one step back and the game continues. If the egg is dropped but not broken, the teammate may pick it up and throw it back—and consider themselves lucky!

My tip: Have a hose ready for cleanup!

Make Goop: Goop is like Silly Putty that stretches into all kinds of dangling shapes. Something about maneuvering it this way and that can fascinate your kids for hours. It's also easy to make!

My tip: use this activity strategically, like on days when everyone is stuck inside or when you may have neglected to plan. You'll find a great Rubbery Goop recipe on Learning4kids.net.

DON'T WAIT; DO IT NOW!

My final tip on formal activities is to do them now, during the elementary stage. When they reach the older stages, there will be little interest in games and outings, and your influence will be limited.

> **Get involved in as many of your child's activities as possible—in fact, suck the very life out of it now, before it's too late.**

The elementary years still provide opportunities to get involved in your child's life. Once these years are gone, the opportunities to be in their world dry up. Room mothers and field-trip chaperones aren't required in the older stages. Get involved in as many of your child's activities as possible—in fact, suck the very life out of it now, before it's too late.

SCHOOL INVOLVEMENT—THE MANY-FACETED SOLUTION

Getting involved in your child's elementary school isn't only a great way to stay relevant in their life, but it's also an amazing way to get to know people. I made many quality friendships through my school involvement. My boys loved it too because I always had the intel on what was being served or what party games were played at the different events. More importantly I also knew some of the family dynamics of my sons' friends because I got to know their parents.

My tip regarding school involvement is to take that call from the room mother, answer that email, sign up as a chaperone, and do it. Some moms feel like their presence would embarrass the child, but I found the opposite to be true: the kids thrived because of my involvement.

• • •

JOURNALING IN THE ELEMENTARY YEARS

ACADEMIC AND SPORTS/ACTIVITY BINDERS

In elementary school, I created academic binders, specific to the boys' academic milestones and achievements. I used pocket folders so I could separate them out by year. For instance, the kindergarten year has their report cards, class photos, any ribbons or awards they received. This goes all the way up to prom: prom pictures, ACT scores, diplomas, etc. This is no small book. I used a five-inch binder for each child, and they are packed full.

At the same time that they began having academic memories, they began joining sports teams. This created a separate need for organization, so I created sports/activity binders. In these binders I have every team photo, covered in plastic, photos of the banners we made when I was team mom, and the pool and birthday parties we had with the teams. I added quite a bit of written detail to the books as well, so it's like reading the story of each child's academic and activity life.

My tip? Get your hands on a few five-inch binders. Shutterfly is outstanding for photos, but these binders will house actual memorabilia, like report cards, scores, ribbons, etc. You'll need the space these large binders provide.

CHAPTER 6

MIDDLE SCHOOL STAGE (AGES ELEVEN TO THIRTEEN)

During the middle school years, from eleven to thirteen years of age, you're still building a foundation, although your child's attitude may make you feel nothing but chaos is being achieved. In fact you are still building, because the preteen can't drive and remove himself from your rules yet. That stage is coming! So this transition stage, although shorter, more awkward, and seemingly less important, is your last chance to make your values impactful.

THE ALIENS HAVE LANDED

Somewhere during the middle school phase with our second son, Scott and I identified a pattern. It's like someone removed our child from their body and replaced them with a new, mouthy version who doesn't want to be with or do things with the family. We had a code phrase for this time of life that usually started with, "Shit … The aliens have landed."

One particular incident during this stage stands out to me. We had taken a trip to Costa Rica, and our package included two villas next to each other. The boys were old enough at this point to handle staying in one, so we stayed in the other.

This should have been a week filled with relaxation and exciting new things to explore. Instead, one person—just one—turned every relaxation point to stress, every new adventure into a bummer, and this one person ruined everyone's time for the duration of the trip. Avery, in the full throes of alien abduction, expertly succeeded at this through sheer middle-school-stage attitude alone.

He demanded the largest room in their villa, declaring it off limits to his brothers, and just oozed alien attitude. Not only did this create bickering and fighting, but it also left the three others to share two beds.

It sounds like I should have been able to demand different behavior, doesn't it? I mean up until this point, I've given tip after tip that has worked over and over. This is exactly what you need to pay attention to because the middle school stage will do this to you if you're not prepared. (And sometimes when you think you are prepared!)

The emotions that swirl during these upsets affect you as the parent as much as the child. You're still trying to find your sweet baby, and they're just not in there. Meanwhile you have to consider all the emotions, arguments, and points of view of all other family members. All you want at this moment is for your kid to go back to normal, and "normal" is a path forward with this type of upset driving the house. In the end we did make him share the room, but the lingering attitude and moodiness were toxic.

Another incident of middle school swirling emotions that stands out happened with Ryan. He was pitcher for an important game, and his team lost. He felt the circumstances surrounding the loss were unfair—and maybe he had a point. However, in ninety-degree heat, after playing in the Houston sun all evening, he decided he was going to walk home, presumably needing to physically move in order to deal with his anger. We didn't like it, but we let him go for it. He needed his time to sort through his emotions and be alone.

I can give you tips on handling this stage, but truthfully as a mom with a heart for your kids, it may take some discipline of your own to carry through.

CONSISTENCY + CONSEQUENCES = EFFECTIVENESS

Throughout all the stages, as mentioned, consistency and sticking to your guns will produce the best long-term results. In the middle school stage, you want to add clear consequences to this consistency. For example, let's say your rule is that nobody leaves the table until everyone is finished eating. Your thirteen-year-old, who's feeling very brave these days, just launches off their chair when they're done, ignoring the rule completely.

The consistent parent in you will immediately correct the behavior, insisting that the preteen return to the table, per the rules they've lived by their entire life.

Now comes your middle schooler's new and definitely unimproved response. They don't see why it's necessary to observe this rule. "It's always been a dumb rule; so-and-so eats too slow; I can't stand just sitting here." The eyes they turn on you are so full of rebellion it can almost scare you.

Shore up your strength, and don't cave to that. Don't start a fight; don't engage in their anger. Moms, especially, you will actually both understand this tantrum and want to backhand them for displaying it, all at the same time. Don't go that route either! Simply arm yourself with consequences, and calmly state what it will be: "Please sit at the table until everyone is done, or you will not be going out with your team after the game tonight." Bam!

When it comes to consequences, make sure the punishment fits the crime, it counts, and you can enforce it.

When it comes to consequences, make sure the punishment fits the crime, it counts, and you can enforce it. Let's take a closer look at these three criteria for enforcing your rules via consequences:

1. **Make Sure the Punishment Fits the Crime:** Rudely leaving the table is certainly an unwelcomed offense, but it's not worth, say, grounding them from the family vacation over it. Missing out on a fun event *that's happening that night* fits the crime much better and will have an immediate effect. *(It's always best when repercussions happen very soon!)*

2. **Make the Punishment Count:** Don't let any "feel-sorry-for-them" tendencies get ahold of you here. You know the party after the game is important to them. *That's why it's the consequence.* State it clearly, with as little drama on your part as possible, and force yourself, if needed, to carry through. They are still young enough for crocodile tears at this stage, so guard against it. Tears don't mean your baby is back; tears

mean the aliens have sent their hormones on another roller coaster. If you give in to them, you will set a precedent you'll have a hard time reversing.

3. **Make Sure You Can Enforce the Punishment:** To discipline the above situation by saying something like, "Get back here, or you'll have dish duty tonight!" isn't effective *because you don't really control whether they'll listen.* They can come back at you and say, "Oh no, I'm not! I'm never doing dishes again!"

At this stage they go where you take them, and if you say we're going home after the game, it's a real consequence because *you're driving,* therefore *you have the power* to enforce it.

Perhaps my number-one tip for dealing with this age group is to always—even if you have to think ahead and make a list of meaningful, effective punishments—*always keep the power of enforcing the punishment in your control!*

YOUR UNDERSTANDING IS IMPORTANT

Although your new mom superpower is toughness, always retain that instinctive understanding of your child. Is there a reason for the emotional outburst? Has there been a breakup? Are they not feeling well? Are they struggling with body issues or peer pressure? Take time to find out, and carefully explain that feeling negative emotions is part of life, but treating others properly is still a requirement, no matter what.

Think about later in life, if someone on the job is rude to them or they don't get that promotion or they have a coworker that just irks them. What if they lack emotional control and start screaming, swearing, and pouting then? First an adult who acts this way is

SWEETIE, SQUEEZE YOUR CHEEKS

instantly laughed at and judged. Second they probably won't last very long at the job because these types of outbursts justify their dismissal.

My tip: understand your child, but don't allow them to be rude. Teach them, through your understanding, what is acceptable and unacceptable behavior.

THE SEX TALK IN THE MIDDLE SCHOOL STAGE

Sex talks during this stage become ever more important because your preteen's body is capable of reproducing, and some middle schoolers are sexually active at this stage. If that makes you cringe, you're not alone, and one way to keep that from being your middle school child's experience is to be sure to talk with them about sex openly and early. Pregnancy will ruin their lives. You must overcome any embarrassment or hang-ups you may have about talking to them about it. You don't want a life-changing misstep to happen at this stage or any other.

What exactly do you tell them at this age? Glad you asked! Here are a few conversations I prioritized with my sons. Parents of girls, please feel free to adjust these conversations for your daughters:

Different Guy/Girl Mindsets: At this stage I was careful to bring up the different ways that girls and guys feel about, or respond to, sex. Both boys and girls need to know that sex for a girl is very emotional and bonding, but it can be purely physical for a young man at this age.

Reputations: I was careful to explain that a girl's reputation is very important, so never talk about what's done in private. Even if the girl has already been with a few guys, be the one that gives her respect, because she may not have much self-esteem.

*If you have daughters, tell them clearly that they can wait, and yes, boys still respect a girl today who says, "No."

"No" Means No! Speaking of saying no, again because I raised sons, I was clear about explaining that boys are typically physically stronger than girls. Also, an impassioned young man's brain is barely functioning, and his body may try to lead without considering the girl. I explained that it's wrong, abhorrent, to force oneself on a girl. If she says, "No," then that means no! Back off!

Pregnancy: Discussing the very real ramifications of a pregnancy is an obvious must during sex talks. I painted a pretty graphic picture at this age, trying to scare them, because we all know only a few emotions will reach a passionate haze, and fear is one of them.

I'd caution them to always take the responsibility to wear a condom, and never, ever leave the birth control exclusively to the girl. Why not? Because even if you're inseparable and she's completely trustworthy, you don't know if she's faithfully taken her birth control without missing any days at all. One or two missed days earlier that month can be easily forgotten about when they're in the moment.

A pregnancy at any point before they are adults—hopefully happily married—will ruin their lives, but at this stage the scars can last forever. Talk openly with your kids; let them learn about sex from you, their life guides, not from a movie or, worse, their friends.

BE THE ONE THEY TALK TO

Many parents may be uncomfortable, even negatively judgmental regarding just how open I was with my middle schoolers about sex. Besides showing them gross pictures of VD at the elementary stage, I took them to Walgreens during the middle school years and clearly showed them the condom aisle. I tried not to completely mortify them right there in the store, but I did explain that there are different sizes, colors, and textures, and to be effective it's critical that one fits properly. Especially when I knew that they had girlfriends, I let it be known that I'd purchase condoms for them if needed.

If you're shocked and offended by that, try to see it from this viewpoint: nature will take its course, and I knew more than they did what kind of nightmare VD or pregnancy would cause them. That nightmare "shocked and offended" me right to Walgreens with every single one of them.

I tackled every subject, from feelings to masturbation to penile irritation from "too much rubbing." In fact when Ryan was in this stage, we went on a cruise filled with other families with similar-aged kids. Us parents were all fairly lenient with our curfews during this trip because, I mean, the kids are on a ship in the middle of the ocean; most every activity is supervised, and there's nowhere else for them to go.

It was about eight o'clock at night, and Ryan (then twelve) asked if he could go in one of the hot tubs with a group he had met on the trip. After verifying which hot tub he was referring to—the one by the kiddie pool—we told him he could go, but he needed to be back by eleven o'clock. Off he went.

When he returned at eleven, he went to Scott with a problem. He said, "Dad, the tip of my penis hurts; you got any Neosporin?"

This was an alarming statement, as you can imagine, so Scott jumped up and responded concernedly, "What's going on? Let me see it."

Turns out there was a girl (age thirteen) in the hot tub with Ryan, and apparently extensive rubbing went on through the mesh of his swimsuit. The hot water only aggravated the situation, and he basically had a pretty bad brush burn on his penis. It was severe enough that they had to tell me about it. (I mean who else would really have the Neosporin?)

I explained that the mesh, especially in water temperatures that high, caused friction. This is something you want to avoid, especially in such a sensitive area. I then gave him the Neosporin he asked for.

As I mentioned, this age group begins to be sexually active. Awareness of the penis and the vagina, and exactly how they fit together, begins early!

Here is my tip: parents, in these types of situations, it's important to remain calm and remember you are their support. Be the one they go to and talk to about any problem they have.

THE NOT-SO-SUBTLE CHANGE IN INFLUENCE

This may be the most bothersome part of parenting the middle school age group. It's when they stop looking to you as their main influence, and they give that all-important status to those who obviously know best—their friends. Be prepared for all five stages of grief, because you will experience each one: denial, anger, bargaining, depression, and finally a form of acceptance.

While you're processing that emotional tidal wave, you must act with consistency and rationality. That's why you start in the younger stages, prioritizing things like family values, quality time together as a unit, education, respect for others and self, regular meals at the table, weekly talks, sports/formal physical activity, good hygiene, and chores. At this time you want to continue enforcing those priorities as if your middle schooler doesn't have any other option.

My tip here, again, is to remain consistent. If you had a standing date for Friday night family movie night for the past thirteen years, it's expected that they still attend. If you're lucky they won't even question it.

On the reasonable side, if possible, have that home where friends hang out. This is the best way to keep some sort of grip on exactly how your kids' friends are influencing them and with what.

A huge tip here would be to make sure you or a responsible adult is home and actively supervising if yours is the hangout home. Don't be the home where the kids hang out because there is no parental supervision. You know what happens in that house!

My last tip for this phase of the middle school stage is to set a "one-night-for-family, one-night-for-friends" rule now. This means they're only allowed to spend time "out with friends" one night of the weekend. Why? The high school stage is coming soon, and if there is no rule in place, they'll be out from Friday to Sunday, and you will rarely see them—or influence them—at all.

CELL PHONES: TIME FOR A CONTRACT

In the middle school stage, sadly, kids are likely to have their own cell phone, and everything changes. I know, using a cell is an everyday experience, but this little device opens up the entire world to your innocent eleven-to-thirteen-year-old. Kids need to understand the importance of being responsible with something that will make a forever record of everything they do on it. Cell phones can be the vehicle for such disasters as credit-card theft, stalking/tracking, and private conversations with predators that parents cannot hear. A high level of responsibility is needed for them to use something so powerful.

So yes, we did create contracts for their cell phone use and for their social media use as well. Developing a contract makes me think about discussion points that need to be addressed. I'll include some samples at the end of the section, but the biggest points we tried to burn into their brains were these:

1. Since their name isn't on the contract and they don't pay the bill, they don't own the phones. We do. Since the phone is in their father's name, he's responsible for what's on them, even if he has no idea of, or connection to, how it got there. If they put illegal photos of any kind on their phone, their dad could get in trouble.

2. In our household, no TVs, computers, or phones are allowed in the bedrooms. Specifically, phones need to be left in the kitchen on the charger.

Lo and behold, our eighteen-year-old's phone kept disappearing off the counter. The next morning I would say something like, "Reece, Dad and I noticed your phone was missing last night ..."

And he would always make up an excuse: "Oh, I fell asleep," or "I was too lazy to go downstairs and connect it."

Of course, Dawson, our sixteen-year-old, was watching and listening to all this, so we had to follow through and be consistent. We said, "Look, Reece, in four months, you'll be off at college and we won't be there, so you can sleep with the phone right there next to your bed if you want to. Until then you have to leave your phone charging on the counter, and if you remove it again and say you 'forgot,' the consequence will be to take your phone for a day."

Gasp, I might have said I was going to remove an arm. No yelling or screaming was necessary, and since then we haven't had any further trouble with forgetfulness—amazing how that works. *(Keep the punishment in your control!)*

1. They had to share their log-on and password keys with us so we could regularly check the phone. They knew I had access to learning who they were really friends with. How does this person text? Is every other phrase, "F-you, bitch"?

If they were replying with like language, they knew I'd see it. If they tried to make derogatory remarks about someone, I corrected them.

2. Regarding texts they had to acknowledge that anything texted is forever and permanent and will never go away. I regularly told them never to text anything they wouldn't say directly to someone's face. They were also asked not to delete any texts among friends. If they are deleting, then there is a concern.

3. If they were old enough for a phone, they were old enough to act with manners and maturity. There are certain times when a sit-down conversation with someone is more appropriate than calling or texting, and breakups fall into this category. I counseled my sons never to break up with a girl by text. The relationship deserves more respect than that.

> **They had to acknowledge that anything texted is forever and permanent and will never go away.**

4. There is a monetary value to this device, and my policy is that if they fall into the pool with it or mishandle it and this results in a broken phone, they are responsible to pay for repairs. Did they drop the phone, and now they have a cracked screen? The fix-it shop is right down the street. Better save up some money because it'll likely be a $500 bill.

ROLE MODELING SAFE CELL PHONE USE

I'll be honest about it: probably the hardest role modeling for me is ignoring my cell phone while driving. It's so easy to grab it and check a quick message at a red light or try to set the GPS while en route to my location. Using a cell phone while driving is especially dangerous for teens and anyone else out on the road. Consequences can be catastrophic and change lives forever. Here are my best tips for role modeling good cell phone safety.

1. Pull over to make any calls or texts or to perform any searches.

2. Use Bluetooth to take calls hands-free.

3. Put the phone on the opposite side of the vehicle so you have to pull over to reach it in order to use it.

4. Get one of the many apps available that will silence your phone and send a message to the caller that you're driving and cannot take their call. (I like this because you never even get tempted by the captivating sound of your ringtone.)

• • •

Safely having a cell phone requires a large amount of responsibility, and my tip is to make them see that. Here is our sample contract for cell phone use:

Sample Phone Contract

1. It is our phone. We bought it. We pay for it. We are loaning it to you.

2. We must always know the password. Never give your password to any friends. If you change your password, you must let us know.

3. If the phone rings, answer it. It is a phone. Say hello, use your manners. Don't ever ignore a phone call if the screen reads "Mom" or "Dad" or "Grandparents." Not ever.

4. No phones at the kitchen table, ever!!!!! Look at it and leave it in another room before coming to eat.

5. You should never be on your phone for large increments of time. (For example: Reading phone for longer than 30 minutes.) Check it, respond, and move on to something else. Charge it when not in use. And always place it in the same place so that you don't forget where you left it.

6. Always charge your phone in the kitchen. Always make sure you're fully charged before leaving home. If you sleep out, make sure you take a charger with you.

7. During school time, you may check your phone before beginning homework. Once homework begins, it stays charging in mom's office. When done with homework, you may check it quickly before retiring to bed.

8. Have a conversation with the people you text in person. It is a life skill. Always look them in the eye.

9. If your phone falls in a toilet, smashes on the ground, or vanishes into thin air, you're responsible for the replacement costs or repairs. Mow a lawn, babysit, take out stash birthday money. It will happen, so you should be prepared.

10. Don't use this technology to lie, fool, or deceive another human being. Don't involve yourself in conversations that are hurtful to others. Be a good friend first. Texting, Snapchatting, emailing, and posting on

Instagram can all get you in trouble if not used correctly. If you ever fear for someone else's life, come to us at once. We'll sit and figure something out.

11. Remember other parents are always watching and reading their children's phone. Use appropriate language at all times.

12. Don't send or receive pictures of your private parts or anyone else's private parts. Don't laugh. Someday you will be tempted to do this despite your high intelligence. It is risky and could ruin your teen/college/adult life. It is hard to make anything of this magnitude disappear—including a bad reputation.

13. Don't take a zillion pictures and videos. There is no need to document everything. Live your experiences. They will be stored in your memory forever. Life is all about experiences. Take the time to sit and delete photos and videos that did not turn out good.

14. Place your phone on silence or vibrate, put it away in public. Especially, in a restaurant, at the movies, or while speaking to another human being. You're not a rude person, don't allow the iPhone to change that. Check your phone many times when away from home in case we need to contact you.

15. If we text you, we expect a text right back. It is rude and unacceptable not to acknowledge the text.

16. Download music that is new or classic or different than your peers. Take advantage of that gift. Expand your horizons.

17. Play a game with words or puzzles or brain teasers every now and then.

18. Keep your eyes up. See the world happening around you. Stare out a window. Listen to the birds. Take a walk. Wonder without googling.

19. You will mess up. We'll take away your phone. We'll sit down and talk about it. We'll start over again. You and I, we are always learning.

20. We are on your team. We are in this together. We love you very much.

With a phone, comes many rules and responsibilities. Please reread this over and over, and keep it in your desk area. Refer to it when needed. Please let us know if there is something we missed that should be added.

We love you very much!
Mommy and Daddy

The following contract was modified specifically for Instagram/ social media sites they would access with this phone. We found it necessary to add this to the mix!

Sample Instagram/Social Media Contract

1. Parents must know your password to Instagram at all times.

2. When parents ask to see your Instagram, it is their right since they own the phone.

3. Don't EVER post inappropriate language or nudity of yourself or others.

4. Don't use Instagram to make yourself popular. Instagram is a tool to keep in touch with others that you may not see on a daily basis.

5. Don't brag when writing your hashtags-make it appropriate.

6. This platform is for you to stay connected with your friends that are close and far (ex: camp friends or Chilean family).

7. Always remain private and don't EVER give out private information like address, phone number, or school.

8. Don't accept anyone onto your account unless you're a 100% sure you know who they are. If not, this will connect you to a whole other world. You don't need to have 2,000 followers.

9. Texting, Snapchatting, and posting on Instagram can all get you in trouble if not used correctly. If you ever fear for someone's life or know of someone posting really bad things (suicide talk, drug talk, Juul videos) you must let US know. If we find out that you did not share this information, your phone gets taken away for exactly 7 days.

10. Remember, 75% of the other parents are connected to their kids' Instagram accounts and will read what you post to your friends' accounts, and they'll see or how you respond to photos and messages. Always be positive when commenting. "If you don't have something good to say, then don't say it." Assume your friends will send anything you post to CNN. Would you be proud of your post if it was on TV?

11. Don't take a zillion pictures and videos. Use this less than more. There is no need to document everything and then post it. Live your experiences.

Be selective in what you post. Life is all about experiences.

12. Once it is posted, it is there for the world to see and read and JUDGE you. Take your time before posting. (For example, it's never a good idea to post while at a party. Take it home and think about it, and when you're ready to post the right picture and hashtag, then you post it.)

13. Any post of any family members must be approved by Mom and Dad first.

If any of the above-stated items are not followed through, you will get your phone taken away and your Instagram deleted. Your parents will decide whether or not you should continue using Instagram or get your phone taken away, depending on the severity.

THEY'RE SNEAKY *AND* SMART—BE SMARTER!

You might think with all these discussions and the formality of signing a contract that my kids would be cautious—if not outright fearful—about straying from acceptable cell phone use. Scott and I were certainly under that impression. Cells were placed on the counter every night; it wasn't a secret that we snooped; and when we did, we saw only approved apps. You won't believe what happened to launch us into a state of awareness.

I received a phone call from the mom of a fellow student in my son's class. The mom, seemingly without any insight as to what this could be about, told me that her son was crying because he wanted a photo "of a girl" that my son had on his phone. The problem, apparently, was that my son hadn't shared it with him.

Alarm bells were ripping through me as my own awareness put together exactly what type of photo this might be. That the other mom was showing signs of complete noncomprehension was both bewildering and comforting at this moment. She didn't see a problem, so I thanked her and reassured her that I'd check into it.

My first course of action was to tell Scott what was going on. With a united front, we called Ryan into our bedroom. When we asked him what "picture of a girl" could be making a classmate so upset, his answer had Scott and me looking over at each other for support. Fidgeting and obviously wanting to get out of that conversation, he finally explained that yes, he did have nude photos of girls on his phone. The young ladies themselves had sent them to him—apparently this is common among this age group! (Talk about things to be aware of!)

When we asked, astounded, how he had something like that on his phone without us knowing, he further educated us on a nifty little app called a photo vault, located behind his calculator app. This app is designed to allow someone to have a folder of secret photos hidden on their phone. Inside this app was the photo his classmate was "desperate" for.

Moms and dads, there will be moments when the actions of your kids demand everything you've got to parent them. He knew he committed a serious breach of rules. For this he was grounded from his phone as the contract states. The worst punishment for him, it seemed, was that we made him delete the photo vault right in front of us. (That look of anguish ... good grief, boys at that age!)

I knew then that the way this was handled would make or break the way he felt about confiding in us ever again. I explained that it was natural to want to look at girls, but photos like those were considered pornographic, which was against the law and against our rules. I further explained that if he wanted to look at a naked photo, it was critically important, for both legal and moral reasons, to delete it and never forward it around. (Thank God that Mom reached out before that happened!)

I feel like the understanding and consequences offered in this situation created a closeness between my son and me that lasted well into his high school years. The last thing I wanted was for him to feel wrong in any way for wanting to see a naked girl. Worse, I didn't want him to clam up and begin distrusting the safe space of our open dialogues.

My final tip for this section is to stay up as much as possible on the new technology, apps, and what social media experiences are available to your preteen. (It's exhausting!) They are good kids, but they have no problem at this age being tricky to get what they want. To retain any type of authority and respect, you must be smarter than them!

• • •

The middle school stage really is somewhat of a transition stage. Your baby is growing up, and they have options regarding how they spend their time. You may feel a tug-of-war beginning where you're pulling one way and friends are pulling the other. Take a deep breath, and get a firm hold of your end of the rope, because the problems in the next stage can literally mean life or death. They are entering the high school years.

• • •

JOURNALING IN THE MIDDLE SCHOOL STAGE

ORGANIZATION AND UPKEEP OF MEMORIES

By now if you've created journals and photo binders, you will have baby books, academic binders, and sports/activity binders piling up. How in the world does a busy mom keep it all organized? The answer: Pendaflex Expansion Pocket Folders, clearly marked with each child's name.

These folders provide several pockets to file different items, so when they brought home, say, ACT scores or junior-high photos, I had a quick and easy way to organize each item. Then when I had some free time, I'd place them in their permanent binder. I'm envious of moms today who streamline this process with photo logs right in their cell phones or through Shutterfly.

In my case, because videos during that time were all on DVDs, I had a professional put our home movies on thumb drives in chronological order. It begins in 1993, when Scott and I got married, and moves through all our family vacations and favorite memories, like a movie of our life together. It is so amazing that I had one made for each of our sons.

Here's my tip for organization and upkeep of your memories: keep all your memories in chronological order to create a "book" of your child's life.

CHAPTER 7

THE HIGH SCHOOL YEARS (AGES FOURTEEN TO EIGHTEEN)

The differences between a middle schooler and a high schooler are vast, even though the actual time lapse is only a couple of years. In the middle school years, you still get glimpses of your baby. In the high school years, your baby is officially gone, and all the training you've put in is now in a form of freefall. It's the toughest of all the stages, and there will be times when you wonder if anything you taught them ever actually stuck.

An example of this drastic change between these stages occurred in my home when Reece was about fifteen and Dawson was twelve. Now these two had always played, fought, and done life together on a somewhat even physical scale. I mean three years in the baby stages is a lot of difference in growth, but they were always pretty much at the same general level of "baby strength."

Dawson at this point hadn't entered puberty yet. He was still just like a dangling green bean that would fall over if you exhaled with too much force. Reece, on the other hand, was a high schooler in full-blown puberty. He didn't understand the developing strength in his own body and that his brother was now at a different physical place than he was. Here's what happened, verified in detail by Ada (my mom).

One night I had a lasagna in the oven, my mom had just gotten a new car and was coming to show us, and we were planning a nice dinner together as a family. Mom, who the boys called Ada, pulled up to the house just as the lasagna was finishing up, so I sent everyone outside to see the new car. You know that feeling you get when you're trying to cook and the kitchen is hectic, then everyone leaves and you get a moment of peace? I had that feeling for exactly five minutes when bam!

As the boys were checking out Ada's new ride, Dawson began chiding Reece about something silly. Well, Reece didn't like it, and he turned around and warned his brother to stop. As brothers will do, Dawson challenged Reece by not only saying the phrase again but also continuing to say it in a mocking way.

Reece snapped and started chasing his brother, just like they'd always done.

It usually ended in a harmless-but-effective punch that reestablished the pecking order. However, they were in different stages now, and Reece's new testosterone-filled bulk didn't throw easy punches anymore.

Seeing his brother start to chase him, Dawson started running toward the grass, not comprehending his brother's physical differences any more than Reece did. He decided to turn and do a playful, taunting backward run just as his feet cleared the driveway and the grass began. Reece was right on his heels, though, and when he pushed Dawson, the force was stronger than he meant it to be. Dawson crashed to the ground, all his weight landing on his shoulder, and snap went his collarbone.

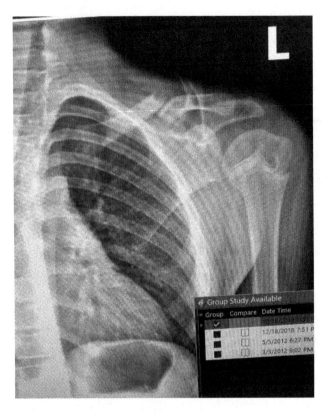

Dawson's collarbone.

As I was setting the lasagna on the stove, Dawson came in screaming, his right shoulder up around his ear in a grotesquely unnatural angle. When I saw it, I screamed so loud, not just at the sight but in anger. The look of guilt on Reece's face was pronounced as, shaking, he confessed it all. I knew he hadn't meant things to get this out of hand, but now I had an unexpected trip to the ER on my schedule. It took us twenty minutes to get Dawson in the car, because his bones kept rubbing together and causing him agony.

Hormones are impacting them in the high school stage, dramatically. For boys this hormonal assault results in competitiveness and physical expenditures of their energy. For girls it's the eye rolling and petty insults. Either way, you have entered the most difficult stage of parenting.

BIGGER KIDS, BIGGER PROBLEMS

The hormonal changes that we are talking about can send high schoolers on truly dangerous paths during this stage. Pregnancy, drug use, unsafe driving, and parties where these hormones are raging are everyday possibilities in the high school years. Frankly parents in the younger stages don't understand the phrase, "Bigger kids, bigger problems; smaller kids, smaller problems." Each stage of motherhood makes you think it's the hardest, until you get here. Then you'll wish for those "small" problems, like potty training and lack of sleep. Here are my four best tips for the bigger issues you and they may face in the high school years:

Sex and Relationships: At this phase it's important to continually reiterate the necessity for safe sex and condom use. Real relationships may be added to the mix to complicate everything. Sex isn't just some foreign concept; it may be a reality, and real feelings are involved. If you ever have to watch your child go through a breakup, you'll feel it with them just as if you were being jilted.

My tip for talking to them about sex in this stage is to create realistic scenarios that they can relate to, like this: "Always remember to wear a condom, no matter what. You know, college is around the corner, and you might be hammered from some party, maybe with a longtime girlfriend, and you lose your sense of caution. Never let that happen. Always use a condom."

All you can do is hope that if they're ever in such a situation, your words come back to haunt—I mean, guide—them.

Random Drug Testing: Your local drugstore/grocery store carries drug-testing kits for weed, nicotine, alcohol, and even hard drugs like heroin or cocaine. I recommend having whatever type you feel you need on hand and openly letting your teenagers know that they'll be tested randomly.

Dawson recently took a trip to Canada, and he was with kids from all over the world, from all walks of life. I truly didn't feel he was interested in vaping, but he was going on a trip with a bunch of people that may want to peer pressure him into it. He may want to fit in and try it—because this vaping thing is currently out of control. I cautioned him straight up: "I want you to know you'll be tested when you return." For impact I plopped the big, blue nicotine-test box right down in front of him.

Now he'd seen his three older brothers go through this, so it wasn't a shock. He replied with a bit of an exasperated, "Mom ... I don't vape!"

I continued the conversation by saying, "I still need to hold you accountable. And if someone tries to push you, blame me. Say, 'Hey my parents are drug testing me when I get home, and it's not worth losing my phone or having the car taken away over vaping.'"

My tip here is to keep those drug tests out in plain view. Why?

Actually it's to help them. When friends come over, they see it, clear as day, and they know my sons are serious when they blame us.

I've heard friends ask, "What's that?"

Usually, I'll tell them, straight out, "It's a nicotine test. We do random drug tests at our house."

The point is to take the heat of the situation off your teen and put it on yourself. Yes, we want them to be strong leaders who can say no to peer pressure, but this is a tough time of life. Nothing wrong with bearing some of their pressure on your shoulders.

Driving Contracts: Possibly one of the most frightening aspects of the high school stage is when they become licensed drivers—an absolutely perfect time for a contract!

Two weeks before I wrote this chapter, Dawson started driving, and we presented him his driving contract. He had seen this three times before, and yet the first thing he wanted to verify was if his brothers had gotten the same driving contract. Why, yes indeed, they did! As a car or truck weighs about five-thousand-plus pounds and travels at high speeds, it can be a killing machine. Vehicles must be operated soberly and cautiously.

We also stressed safety once a vehicle is parked, not to leave laptops or other valuables on the seat where thieves can see them. We explained what to do if they were ever pulled over by the police, etc. I'll admit, we heard some complaints, like, "Y'all are over the top; there are contracts for everything in this house!" I do look back and chuckle at myself. However, if I had to do it again today, I would still create contracts. Why? Everything is very clear on the contracts, and as we mentioned earlier in the book, part of receiving it is the discussion around each point.

The day I began this very chapter, Dawson, the new driver, called me: "Mom, when can I drive on the freeways?"

"Well, that's clear as day in your contract [smug smile]. When you get home, we'll have to review it."

My tip here is to go over the contract regularly. This should be a sit-down, relaxed discussion that reinforces each point. Here is our sample driving contract:

Driving Contract

1. You must always let us know where you are going, who you are going with, and when you will be arriving home.
2.
3. Your curfew is 11:30 PM, but note, we also have the right to change the time depending on the situation, which means we can make it 10:00 PM.
4.
5. When arriving home at NIGHT, you must ALWAYS wake your mother or father to say, "Hello, I am home."
6.
7. You must always know exactly where you are going and how to get there **BEFORE** leaving the house.

8. Your phone must always have a "FULL CHARGE" before leaving the house, during the day or night, to drive.

9. You must always text us when leaving and arriving in different places. This is for the first 6 months.

There is no driving on highways of any sort for three months. You may begin driving to school on the highway starting on (Provide specific date, such as July 28th). Driving on the highway is also only on an "as needed" basis.

Never, ever text while driving or check texts while the car is running. No talking on the phone while driving either. If it is that important, stop and park to call or text.

When passengers are in the car the music is to remain low. If friends become rowdy in the car and you cannot focus, you must pull over and place hazard lights on and calm everyone down.

You are allowed one friend in the car with you, per the law.

Always have $20 cash in your wallet at all times for emergencies and $5 in your glove compartment box.

Only pump gas during the day and always be mindful of how much gas you have. Be aware of your surroundings while pumping gas, and always lock car doors when pumping gas. Try your best to pump at the Bellaire location.

You should know how to call a wrecker if you need road assistance. (Triple AAA) Have the number and card in your wallet.

You must know what to do if you get stopped by the police. Where is your insurance card? Have your driver's license ready.

At any time if there is a driving ticket or an accident, you will likely lose your driving privilege for a period of time. You will also need to cover some of the car expenses/damages.

Take pride in yourself and your vehicle. Keep the car clean.

Follow the rules and always drive with caution.

Being in a rush is never a good thing, so always leave in plenty of time. There is traffic and construction in our city all the time, so give yourself plenty of time. Better to be early than late.

Ask yourself, "What is that car about to do?" Don't trust any car to do the "right thing" or follow the law because oftentimes they don't. However, you must do the right thing and follow the law. Make us PROUD!

We love you very much. It is not you that we don't trust; it is the other drivers.

Academics Really Count Now: One of the things you have to be on top of during high school is the fact that the minute they hit ninth grade, they are prepping for college. Their grades count, and their attendance and participation in class all go straight into their scores for college consideration.

Dawson, knowing that honors courses boost the college application, applied for an honors class in world history. To his dismay he wasn't automatically accepted but had to go through an interview process to get in. The head of the school sat across from him, looked at him seriously, and said, "I need to know what your study habits are. Why do you feel you should have this honors course?"

My son was caught off guard, but he was able to answer honestly, "I study in my room, but I turn my phone in."

The headmaster sat straight up. "You do what?"

Dawson explained, "I'm not allowed to have my phone in my room or while I'm studying, so my phone stays downstairs."

The headmaster was so impressed with this, he got the credit he needed for the studying portion. After that he was required to show "strength of schedule," which basically means the student isn't milking all the easy classes; their studies are getting progressively harder year after year. He was able to show strength of schedule, and he was finally accepted into the course.

The first thing moms ask me is how I got high schoolers to continue turning in their phone. As I've been saying, it starts when they're small, and it continues because you're consistent. If they know you will give in and get lax on the rules, they'll take the proverbial mile, and it will be difficult to regain your ground. The key really is to start requiring compliance when they're small, before they become disrespectful aliens who feel they should be able to do whatever they want.

My tip: we learned about the importance of the ninth-grade year with Avery and Ryan, so with Reece and Dawson, we streamlined and blended the phone contract with a ninth-grade contract. Here is the example of the blended contract:

> **The key is to start requiring compliance when they're small, before they become disrespectful aliens who feel they should be able to do whatever they want.**

Sample 9th Grade Contract

Grades now count. We expect full effort for each class. Hard work will get you mid to high 90's at your school. If you need tutor help you need to ask us and also aggressively attend ha'shara's.

You are attending a private school, so take advantage of the small class size and getting to know your teachers. The more you visit with them before and after school, the more they will like you and see that you are always trying.

Remember, two teachers at your school will be writing your senior letters for college, so develop a connection with them. This also prepares you for college which is where it's extremely important to have a connection with your professors.

We expect you to be well organized at all times with binders and notes. You must have an agenda, and it must be color coordinated. Set reminders on your phone; USE POST IT NOTES.

Highschool is the time to try different outside activities. Get involved at school. Run for student government, Tikkum Olam, National Honor Society. Start building yourself a resume for your college applications now. Think of where you want to volunteer your time since you MUST turn in hours every April. Get involved!!! Make new friends…don't isolate yourself into one small group.

NO DRUGS OR ALCOHOL: If we suspect, we will test you, and there will be consequences. If we suspect your friends are partaking, then we will also begin randomly drug testing you. Let your peers know that you are drug tested IF THEY PRESSURE YOU TO TRY SOMETHING; it is an easy way out. Or just say "NO." Please don't disappoint us.

PHONE: Phone is to be charged every night on the kitchen counter. There will be random checks of your phone and absolutely no deleting of texts or emails. Remember to reread your contracts about Instagram.
STARTING FRESHMAN YEAR, PHONE NO LONGER GOES UPSTAIRS WITH YOU. IT WILL BE HANDED TO ME. THERE WILL NO LONGER BE FACETIME WHILE DOING

HOMEWORK.

SNAPCHAT: Remain private accounts at all times and never meet random people on social media. You may think it is a pretty girl your age, but it could be a 50-year-old pedophile.

Everything done on Facebook, text, email, Instagram, Snapchat, etc. can be retrieved. Do not post anything you don't want the principal of the school reading. Always remember that other parents (especially girl parents) check their teens' phones. Watch what you type and send. NO CUSS WORDS, EVER!!!

When we email or text you, you must reply promptly. We need to know where you are and where you are going.

We need respect at all times. No raising your voice to us, talking back, insulting, punching, cussing via phone, text, email, and in person. No hanging up on us either. We are your parents and we brought you into this world, so give us a little respect.

You are a role model to your younger siblings/cousins. Be mindful of that when you are with them. You will now be at the same high school as your brother/sister. If you hear things, please be honest and tell us. We are a safe house. He/she is your blood, your family, and we know you love him.

PARTIES: You will be invited to a lot of them, and you will be able to attend if we know where it is taking place and who will be attending. You need to choose one night of the weekend to hang out with family and the other to be with friends. Curfew is 11:00 PM, depending on the situation.

Consequences in breaking our contract will result in being grounded from going out with friends, and your phone will be taken away. Depending on the circumstances, penalties will vary.

Sign:_____

Mom & Dad

PREPARING THEM FOR COLLEGE

College is an expectation in our house, and my kids know it. So, as I mentioned, everything starting in the ninth-grade year is about getting them into the best position for college.

They need to be ready academically, mentally, emotionally, and practically, with some basic self-care skills. You have four years at this point to prepare them. Sounds like more than enough time, right? Trust me, it will take all four years to really prepare them for the leap into the college stage. Here are a few strategies we used to provide them a head start:

USE TUTORS

When high schoolers are on a collegiate path, one low grade can spoil their chances of getting into their preferred college. Because of this when my oldest two sons went through high school, we used professional tutoring services when they needed additional help with a subject. I don't mind telling you that this was getting very expensive. These tutors were charging upward of $120 an hour for their services.

Then this light-bulb moment occurred: the director of admissions at my kids' high school was a friend of mine. These directors know the GPAs of all the students and who is excelling in their studies. What if I hired honor-roll students as tutors? These kids had already been through these courses, sometimes with the same teacher, and came out with stellar grades. They could be more effective than professional tutoring services!

So I called the school and asked the admissions director if she could recommend such a senior who might be looking to make some money. These became our tutors. Hiring these student tutors was the best move we made for the academic side of our lives. For about twenty to thirty dollars an hour, I had specialized tutors, and they were outstanding. They came to my home for an hour a day, and instead of me tearing my hair out trying to help four kids with homework, these tutors took on the bulk of that. The positive benefits were endless:

1. These students didn't have other jobs, so they were flexible. I recall a few later-game nights when our tutor would come in the evening to accommodate our sports schedules. Good luck getting a professional tutor service to do that.

2. When the tutor showed up, it was another, older kid from school. Kids tend not to act up or resist the flow in front of peers in this type of situation. This means the "fight to get them to study" is virtually nonexistent. (It's worth every dollar just to get that benefit!)

3. For the price of one hour of tutoring from a professional service, I literally got an hour of "homework assistance" every weekday. The value to our family was exponentially better!

4. I tried never to cancel a tutoring appointment, but things do come up, and if we had to cancel with a student tutor, there was no additional charge or penalty fee. Professional tutor services almost always have a policy requiring payment for cancellations less than twenty-four to forty-eight hours ahead of an appointment.

5. I stayed somewhat involved and served as the homework supervisor, in a way, and those tutors were another set of capable eyes on everyone's work. Together the tutor and I made sure binders were organized, calendars were checked, tests were planned for with sufficient time to study, and actual checking of homework assignments took place. For instance, let's say Reece wrote an English paper, and he needed someone to check it for clarity and grammatical errors. The tutor would do so and make suggestions—"Hey, you need to redo your intro; it's not flowing well." *(Priceless!)*

6. If time or logistics were ever an issue on a particular day, the tutor, of course, went to the same school my sons did. They were able to use the library after school, if needed. *(Working moms, this might be an option for keeping them busy and getting their homework done while you finish up your workday.)*

   Also, because they went to the same school, they lived relatively close, so if they didn't have a car, it was easy to drive them to and from tutoring appointments.

My final tip is to begin locating your child's tutor during the summer prior to their ninth-grade year. If the tutor is ready to go, this will provide your child the best start to their high school academic career.

LET THEM GO—YOUTH VACATION PROGRAMS

I know some moms who go to pieces when the time comes for the kids to go to college. The stark reality that their teens will be "on their own" for the first time terrifies them. They are worried because their young adult has never been on a plane before. What if they're in Atlanta, and they don't know how to locate their connection gate? What if they're not adjusting well, as they've never been away from home?

All of these realities can and should be addressed well ahead of time, and an excellent way to prepare your teens for these types of challenges is to provide them the opportunity to travel in the high school years. Student travel programs, like West Coast Connections, exist to give your high schooler experience traveling. Not only do high schoolers have enriching life experiences on these trips, but they also learn how to traverse an airport, find their layover gate, and be independent for a few weeks each summer.

Our one stipulation was that our sons go on these trips alone. We wanted them to have the experience of getting away from their peers and those who had preconceived ideas about who they were. We wanted them to look around at a group of thirty-five kids on a bus and decide who they were, who they wanted to be, and which crowd they fit into.

This worked out great for the first three kids, but Dawson had a more difficult time finding a friend group. In fact the group he felt he fit into had all come on the trip together, and they weren't accepting of anyone else joining them. It was a shock to him, as he's typically the leader, and he doesn't go through this type of rejection. (Lessons abound when they're out on their own!)

When it was all said and done, he told us that the experiences and sites they visited on the trip were amazing, but he didn't want to do it alone again because it caused such anxiety. So, as parents must do, we flexed and adjusted our criteria. This year he went with his best friend, Harper, and they had an absolute blast!

We also had the benefit of having good family in Chile, and we took advantage of this traveling opportunity as well. Avery and Ryan each traveled to Chile in their eighth-grade summers and stayed with family. Not only did they develop lasting relationships with cousins, aunts, and uncles, but they also came back speaking fluent Spanish. Win-win-win! Unfortunately, the pandemic prevented us from being able to provide this same experience to Reece and Dawson.

My tip for sending them on trips is to begin "cutting the cord" during the younger stages. We introduced sleepaway camp for a couple of weeks out of every summer, starting at about ten years old. We found this to be an easy way of "pushing them from the nest," so to speak, and reinforcing their own independence.

This is what you want! The high schooler should be on a deliberate path toward independence.

COLLEGE-BOUND ANXIETY

We noticed that the summer before college can bring on some anxiety for college-bound students. Think about it: they are leaving their home, their space, siblings, parents, friends, and possibly going to another state where they'll be thrown into a dorm room with strangers. It's understandable that this can cause feelings of anxiousness. Nevertheless, it can hit you as a parent totally out of the blue and be extremely upsetting. One minute you're looking at bedding for the dorm, and the next your high schooler may be hyperventilating.

My tip is to reassure them in any way possible. If they need gray bedding instead of blue, accommodate them—because small things like that are earth shattering during an anxiety attack. Reassure them that you'll always be there, and then, for the good of your high schooler and you, cut the cord!

YOU'RE ONLY AS HAPPY AS YOUR UNHAPPIEST CHILD

Preparing them for college, in a way, is like handing off the baton of their care into their own hands. If you don't consciously prepare them, you may have months of apprehension and adjustments on your hands from a distressed young adult who is, quite possibly, hours away from home. It's in your best interest to teach them, because you're only as happy as your unhappiest child!

During the boys' high school summers, they were responsible for certain chores. So, by the time they left for college, they were adept at handling the basic areas of self-care. If high schoolers aren't able to comfortably perform the following tasks, at the very least, you must ensure that they become proficient in these areas before they begin college:

1. Cooking basic meals, like pasta, eggs, sandwiches, and use of a grill.

2. Properly sorting and washing clothes.

3. Cleaning a bathroom/toilet.

My tip: spend a good amount of time each summer teaching them these things so that when they go to college, they already know how to do them!

STAYING CLOSE IN THE HIGH SCHOOL YEARS

Staying close to your high schooler can feel like trying to force someone to play a game they just don't want to play. Legitimate things now have their attention, and family time can fall away as a nonpriority if you don't make a point of enforcing it. Here are four ways you can keep that closeness flowing with your precollege teen:

Continue "One Night for Family, One Night for Friends": Remember, this is a strategy meant to keep the family close, but it's also meant to limit the influence friends can have on their lives. Allow them to be with their friends, but continue to stipulate that they reserve one night for family. If you have to, negotiate which night is better for them.

Flex When You Can: I came from an era when speaking to somebody was considered proper. When texting came out, I resisted it for as long as I could. I remember consciously pulling myself out of this thinking (and getting rid of my BlackBerry) because I realized that texting was how teenagers communicated. If I didn't learn how, I might never communicate with them again!

You can be a strong parent, and likely you will have to be in these particular years, but always be flexible when you can!

Share a Hobby: If a particular activity is mutually enjoyable, perhaps a hobby you raised them doing, make a point of engaging in that activity together with your high schooler. I know families that ski together, ride ATVs together, sail together … there's an endless number of hobbies you can share with your teen.

My tip for this point is to consider working out together as a family! The health benefits of exercise are well known, and sharing the routine of going to work out is bonding. When our family goes to the gym, we typically scatter to our different equipment, but it's still a shared routine, and "sharing routine" in the high school years is one of the best ways to stay close.

Parent-Child Vacations/Staycations: We discussed keeping kids close during the younger stages by taking them out for one-on-one meals with you. At the high school level, because they were more mature, we kicked that theory up a notch by taking one-on-one vacations with them. For instance, as I'm preparing this chapter, Scott is whitewater rafting with Reece in Colorado. It's just the two of them, having experiences and making memories that will last a lifetime. Because he's our high schooler, on his last summer break before college, he and I have also planned a one-on-one trip to Mexico just before he leaves.

Vacationing with your kids does not have to be a huge, expensive excursion, either! There are many weekend or day trips that can be made on a budget. Try camping near historical sites, museum visits, or rock climbing at your local Bass Pro Shop. One mom I know takes her kids to a nice hotel now and then and lets them swim and enjoy all the luxurious amenities. Then she provides their favorite snacks, and they watch movies all night—a perfect staycation, only ten minutes from home.

My first tip for parent-child vacations is to use college campus visits as opportunities to share one-on-one trips. You're on the road anyhow, so you may as well see the sights around the campus and familiarize your child with the surroundings, should they attend

> **Use college campus visits as opportunities to share one-on-one trips.**

that school. In the process you get to have new adventures together and make amazing memories at the same time.

My second tip is to hold off on any college campus visits until you know what schools have accepted your student. Scott and I learned this one the hard way when, a bit overzealously, we did a campus visit for nearly every school Avery had an interest in. This is unnecessary! They don't need to visit a school that they may not attend. Wait for their acceptance letters, then visit their top choices only.

KEEPING THEM BUSY IN THE HIGH SCHOOL YEARS

The best way to keep your high schooler close, and safe, is to keep them busy! I am a firm believer in having a full schedule for high schoolers, especially during summer. The more time they have on their hands, the more trouble they will get into, as they will find a way to stay occupied, just not the way you might want them to be.

At this stage they should be consumed by their life's passion, whether sports, music, dance, theater, or another healthy life pursuit. If they don't have an activity to consume their time legitimately, frankly they should be working. Veteran moms will tell you, and it's been proven time and again, that what you sincerely want to avoid are high schoolers having too much time on their hands. Our job is to keep them busy—and tired as well!

EARNING THEIR OWN MONEY

If you want your teen to pursue their passion and stay busy, naturally it's going to get expensive, and they are going to need their own spending money. I know families who simply hand over a credit card to their high schooler with no limit to the amount they can spend. This parenting choice does not teach the young adult anything about budgeting, and it conveys a lack of respect regarding the value of a dollar. Earning their own money in this high school stage is an important element of moving them into becoming productive, independent adults.

I want to quickly add that "earning their own money" does not necessarily mean getting a traditional part-time job, say at Starbucks. Remember the life passions we talked about that should be consuming their time? Well, they can turn those passions around and teach them to younger students for a fee. Here's how we did this!

SPORTS CAMP/BASEBALL LESSONS

I have to give credit for this idea to Avery. We had moved in October 2014, and our new house included a basketball court. A light bulb went on for him in December of 2014, and he felt sure that he could put his sports skills to work and run a sports camp. His idea was to have camp for four hours a day, Monday through Friday, during summers, and teach campers all kinds of sports. I thought the idea had a lot of merit, so I told him to go ahead and organize it.

All our sons got involved in this and learned amazing leadership skills as well as aspects of business that we never could have taught them. There were spreadsheets to generate, campers to find, flyers to create, and accounting to be maintained. Then came the different personalities they encountered: how to deal with a bully, a crybaby, the arrogant child, and the cheater.

Along the same lines, Avery, having that first-born, entrepreneurial spirit, decided to specialize in teaching baseball to younger players. To get his services noticed, he made business cards and handed them out at little league games. He charged thirty dollars per hour to go to the home of the student to teach the proper way to throw, hit, scoop, and catch the ball, as well as proper baserunning technique. Not bad for a teenager!

TUTORING ... RETURN THE FAVOR

Just as we sought out tutors who excelled in their subjects, Ryan thought of offering tutoring services to younger students. He was in advanced math, so tutoring younger algebra students was a breeze for him. To locate students he looked in the school directories, where families post a contact email. He wrote up a short sales pitch that included his fee and gathered his students. He followed the same protocol that his tutors did: he went to the home to work with the student.

My tip: since your high schooler will be going to the home of students in younger classes, you may not know the family environment they will walk into. There's nothing wrong with calling the parents of the student to speak directly to them and get a feel for the home dynamics. It's just a friendly, "Hello, this is Jenn Tiras, Ryan's mom; he tells me he's going to be working with Johnny this Wednesday at three o'clock. I just wanted to confirm the time and location and make sure you'll be at home."

A pleasant conversation should take place with another mom or dad. If you get that uneasy feeling, restrict the tutoring to the school library, or have the tutoring take place in your home.

VOLUNTEERING

Another way I saw tremendous positive growth and kept my high schoolers busy was having them volunteer. Typically, high schools will require community service hours for graduation, and this is a great way for them to get school credit and learn to help others as well.

At one point I realized that my children had no idea that there was a large population of homeless people in Houston. Mind you there are homeless people on every other city block, and yet my children were unaware of their needs. This bothered me a great deal, and I sought out some way of changing that.

As it happened I had a large collection of toiletries from traveling, so every summer I'd get out the brown paper lunch sacks, and the boys and I would do an assembly line, adding some food items and some accessories to each bag. Scott and I kept these in our vehicles, and when we encountered a person seeking help, we gave them each a bag. We still role model this today, and our boys have become very aware of the plight of the less fortunate.

You may be surprised at the different volunteering opportunities that are available for your high schooler to volunteer. At the Nehemiah Center in Houston, our teens read to elementary-aged kids; Reece, specifically, volunteered at Nature Discovery Center, where there were opportunities to interact with various reptiles; and at the Houston Food Bank, they were able to pack and hand out food to those in need.

One of my favorite experiences happened while the kids were volunteering at a local church. Our job was to help assemble the sacks of food and help hand them out. Each sack contained something like one loaf of bread, a jar of peanut butter, and a few cans of vegetables. Families in need lined up down the street to receive these bare essentials. At one point I recall a discussion among all my sons where they truly empathized with the people they had met face-to-face just that day. "Mom," Ryan said, "that's all the food they get for the week?"

My tip? Even if your high schooler is so busy that you don't need to fill their time with more, strongly encourage them to have the enriching life experience of volunteering.

PARENTS, THEY STILL NEED YOU!

Watching your birdies fly the coop, even when they are on what seems to be quality life paths, isn't an easy thing to handle. You must let them become independent adults ... however, they still need you! Continue being that undercurrent of support throughout these years.

When my sons began talking about entrepreneurial ideas, they discussed them with Scott and me. The role we served at that time, specifically, was to encourage them: "Yes, we think it's a great idea." When they saw our positive support, it bolstered their own belief in themselves.

The next thing was to get them thinking: "What's your overall plan? Do you think this fee is fair, or should you charge more or less? What type of gym equipment will be needed? Where will you find the best price on equipment to maximize your profit? If kids will be camping from nine o'clock to one o'clock, will they bring a lunch?"

When all the budgeting, snacks, and necessary gym equipment were in place, I stayed present by checking in all the campers, making sure their parents had signed the legal waiver, collected their money, and made sure we had an emergency contact number. Then I kept an eye on things from a background view.

We work together, and when I can suggest a more streamlined plan or make a call to assist them in getting their flyers noticed, I do. What I don't do is help them set up and/or clean up. The entire program, including those aspects, is on them.

THE WHAT I$ PROGRAM

Just as I took on a major support role in the sports camps, Scott stepped in during Avery's freshman year to develop an idea for his volunteer service hours. Scott's expertise is in the financial field, and it was painfully clear that many students knew nothing about financial basics. So they created a PowerPoint presentation called "What I$." It teaches students things like what a checkbook is, what the difference is between a credit card and a debit card, what a retirement fund is, and how to get college financial aid; then they went to work contacting schools where they could present it. It was so effective that, again, Ryan, Reece, and Dawson also taught the program with Scott throughout high school.

Not only were they volunteering, but they were also learning necessary skills to help them later in life. They made the presentation fun by bringing along small rewards for participation and when questions were answered correctly. All in all the program was a great success. Bonus: when college entrance applications came along just a few months later, this looked outstanding on their profiles.

My tip: check out the PowerPoint on Whatisfinancial.org. Honestly it's even fun for adults to see if they know the practical definitions of the financial basics!

OTHER PARENTS WILL DISAPPOINT YOU

In the high school stage, differences in parenting styles will become glaringly obvious. This is when parents who may have had relatively similar rules in their households now think differently, and you may feel excluded from knowing exactly what's going on in their homes. Parenting styles you may find different from yours include the checked-out parent, the clueless parent, the parent in denial, and the friend parents. Let's take a look at each:

The Checked-Out Parent: This parent knows something unhealthy is going on, but they're done with putting in the effort. Maybe they are on their second marriage, life has kicked them around, and they're tired. For whatever reason they've just checked out.

In Avery's freshman year in high school, we encountered this parenting style. He was going to his first high school party. We gave him the heads up on what to expect and assured him that if he felt uncomfortable or needed a ride home at any point, he could call us—no questions asked.

After maybe one hour of him being at the party, I got a call from Avery. He whispered to me, "Mom, I need you to come pick me up. I am hiding in the bushes at the front of the house, and the cops are here."

I responded immediately, beginning to move for the door as I spoke, "On my way."

When I arrived Avery ran to the car and jumped in the front seat. Two more boys were with him, and I could tell they had had a lot to drink, so I told them I would take them home too. In the car one of the boys began to turn green in the face. (God, no; please hold on!) I ran to my trunk, trying to inventory what I could use for this mess. Thank goodness, a shoebox was lying there—that would do the trick.

I grabbed it in the nick of time and got it right up to his mouth as he began to vomit.

As this was happening, I saw the parent who lived in the home and who presumably allowed this party to take place walk out onto the front lawn. She went on and on about how she had no idea there were so many teens in her home; she didn't know that they were drinking; blah, blah, blah.

Guess what I did? I walked right up to her as she tried to deny any responsibility, and I handed her the shoebox filled with vomit. Yep. Then I drove off. She was completely checked out.

The Clueless Parent: The clueless parents are the ones saying, "Oh, my kids would never say the F-word; they would never try marijuana or drink beer." Meanwhile theirs is the kid passed out under the keg because he won the swearing game.

The Parent in Denial: Similar to the clueless parent, these parents are in denial about what's really going on in the world, and therefore they don't know what's really going on with their teen either. This is the parent denying that their eighteen-year-old is sexually active, when all the signs were clear that she'd been active since fourteen.

The Friend Parent: This is the parent who wants to be best friends with their child and forsake the parenting role. These are the parents who allow alcohol, smoking, and God knows what else at their teenager's parties. Scott and I had an incident with "friend parents" that was so disappointing it hurt and still does today. Here's the story:

It was Mother's Day several years back, and I chose to go out for a nice brunch, have a quiet day as a family, and end it with movie night. Honestly this is my favorite kind of day—except this time a wrench was thrown directly into it.

A good friend of Ryan's had a brother celebrating his sixteenth birthday, and the date fell right on Mother's Day that year. A teen only turns sixteen once, so when Ryan was asked to help set up the party, of course we allowed him to go. Knowing what a "party" meant in this household, we told him to be home by ten o'clock.

His curfew came and went, and Ryan wasn't home. Scott and I looked at each other, alarm bells ringing as we began the text thread: "It's time to come home."

He texted back that he wanted to spend the night there; there were still guests at the party; blah, blah, blah …

The situation escalated to a phone call, during which we clearly told him he couldn't sleep over and that he was to come home right away. Hysterics came from the other end of the phone. Remember, crocodile tears are still available to them on demand, and they are only confirmation of alien abduction. We didn't give in to them, but Ryan seemed to be fighting us tooth and nail, which, of course, made us more suspicious. So, we took it to the next level, and we texted the parents.

Now if parents contact us and ask for assistance in getting their teen to comply with their rules, it's an automatic "Yes." We'll do whatever we can to help them, and most parents agree and would do the same. It's the "Parent Code"! These parents did not react with the same respect. Instead they sided with Ryan, suggesting that we were too strict and we should let him stay. They actually went on to imply that our rules did not convey love to our son. At seventeen years old, he should be able to stay out all night if he wanted to. If we really loved him, we would let go a little and allow him to make his own decision about whether to stay at the party.

Get to know the parents of your kids' friends. Be the one who reaches out.

I'd never heard such convoluted BS, and it was jarring to hear this from a longtime friend. It warranted a phone call, and a phone call followed, during which a huge fight broke out. Let's just say we no longer associate with the couple. The disappointment of that night still stings.

My tip for this section is to get to know the parents of your kids' friends. Be the one who reaches out to extend a simple invitation, like, "Hey, it seems like our kids are really good friends; we're having a barbecue this Sunday, and we'd love for you to stop by so we can meet y'all." Don't be surprised, however, if you encounter parenting styles you're adamantly opposed to. In that case try to have that friend over to your house rather than letting your kid go to theirs.

FINAL TIP FOR THE HIGH SCHOOL YEARS

My final tip for the high school years is to engage your high schooler in conversation when they get home from an outing. Ask relevant questions; require them to turn on the light, sit next to you, and tell you about their night.

This practice has a way of deterring them from doing anything they can't look you in the eye over.

• • •

Once the aliens abduct your child, the baby never really comes back, but difficult teens, thankfully, grow into themselves, and the volcanic emotions subside. You have reached the end of the most difficult phase of motherhood. In the next you'll see an adult emerge, and everything you put in—good or bad—will manifest itself. Welcome to the college/young adult years.

• • •

JOURNALING IN THE HIGH SCHOOL STAGE
START ENJOYING THE RESULTS OF YOUR EFFORTS

This past April, Scott celebrated his sixtieth birthday. In the very same weekend, Reece was going to prom and Ryan was having his senior mother-son reunion. Talk about a conflict—I didn't want to miss any of it, but after some family discussions, I decided to go to Ryan's mother-son reunion.

If you recall a few chapters back, we talked about "starting a family tradition." We created the tradition of waking the boys up on their birthday with a candle and singing happy birthday.

Well, during this crazy weekend, when family members were scattered, Dawson, who was turning sixteen two weeks later, texted me and asked how Scott liked his coffee. I thought that was an unusual question, but I told him without thinking too much more about it. (Folgers Instant—nasty stuff!)

To our utter shock, on Scott's birthday Dawson made a big breakfast and woke Scott up with a candle, singing happy birthday. I bawled like a baby when I heard this. They really do get it!

It's as you set them free to make their own choices that you will see how much of your influence has really been conveyed. At this stage you get to see the results of your efforts paying off!

CHAPTER 8

COLLEGE/YOUNG ADULT STAGE (AGES EIGHTEEN TO TWENTY-FOUR)

Upon your kids' graduation from high school, you've made it past the worst of the stages—but you're not completely out of the parenting woods yet. Remember, little kids, little problems; big kids …

Your college freshman may still show signs of childishness, while your senior in college is typically all grown up. Somewhere during that time frame, they do mature. While they're getting there, you still may be dealing with the "child" in your young adult. The difference in this stage is the issues that affect them are all serious: boyfriends/girlfriends, jobs, school, etc.

There may be times when you honestly give your parenting everything you know to be right to give, and when the chips fall, you don't know if you made the right parenting decisions. We had an experience like that with Avery during his college selection process.

He was accepted at a few colleges, including the University of Texas, but he was especially interested in Vanderbilt, located twelve hours away in Nashville.

Now Scott is a UT alumnus, and yes, he wanted to see his sons go there and have as much fun as he did while getting a quality education. He talked it up all their lives, really. When the time came, he even took Avery on two tours of UT, directing his attention to their outstanding business school. Nope. Avery clearly stated that he wanted out of Texas.

Here's the issue: we knew that distance and desire to flee were a dangerous combination when starting out. My intuition told me he would regret this decision, yet he was insistent. There was a period of several days when we thought of forcing him to go to UT, but that went directly against the independence we were trying to teach him. Either way college life would bring good days and bad because that's just life. If we forced him to go to one school over another, the minute a bad day occurred, he would blame us for making him go to that school. As much as we just knew the Vanderbilt choice would cause more adjustment than was necessary, we allowed him to make his own decision.

> **Do everything you can to show them the correct path in life, and then be there for them if their decisions let them down.**

Of course, two weeks in, he was having those adjustment pains, and during a particularly difficult call he said, "Why couldn't y'all just be real parents and tell me I needed to go to UT?"

Ouch! No matter how I tried to explain it, he was mad at everything, and parents are such convenient scapegoats!

He did end up getting through this difficult time, as most freshmen do. However, I had to wonder if maybe we had made a bad parenting decision by allowing him to "make an error." I mean this college choice was turning our family's first college send-off into a mess!

Then I got hold of myself and rejected any guilt. Why? We had done everything we could to make him see our points. At the college/young adult stage, that's really all you can do, and then you must let them go!

Here is my tip: do everything you can to show them the correct path in life, and then be there for them if their decisions let them down.

THE COLLEGE GAMES BEGIN

Regarding those good and bad decisions, college games have a way of deleting any attempt at good sense. I knew that in a way, but I was naive about the reality—boy, did I learn.

In 2017 Avery was invited to UT's annual Plato's Party, so he flew in from Vandy and brought Ryan along. No problem; they could handle themselves; they'd been to many college parties by this time. We also knew the brothers were together, so naturally they would look out for each other; right?

Scott and I silenced our incessantly spamming phones with a false sense of security and went to bed. Little did we know a big problem was developing. As expected Avery was drinking, and someone at the party thought it would be great fun to "roofie" him as well, meaning they secretly put a hypnotic drug in his drink. How do we know this? We found out when the hospital tested him. Here's what happened:

Avery was so intoxicated that he pretty much blacked out, tripped on his own boots, and fell at the party. When he did so, he fell forward—and this was no simple fall! Typically when a person falls this way, they instinctively put their hands out to protect themselves. Because Avery had $C16H12FN3O3$ (roofie) in his system, along with a lot of alcohol, he never even tried to put his hands up to break his fall. He crashed like a fallen tree, face first, right into the cement.

Ryan was there, though! He'd take care of Avery if anything serious was up; right? Turns out not if he's with a girl. Pulling himself away from her, Ryan looked Avery over, saw a little blood from the cheek area, and sent him back to their room in an Uber!

By the time Avery got back, the alcohol was wearing off, and his face hurt—everywhere. He went to the bathroom and got a good look at himself in the mirror. You know how you sort of test your jaw sometimes, and it only moves comfortably about an inch or so? Well the whole bottom of Avery's face moved side to side, completely disconnected from the top half. When he fell he broke both mandibles.

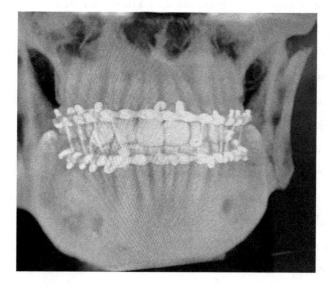

Avery's broken jaw.

Scott woke up at six-thirty that morning, and when he saw all the missed calls and texts, he immediately sprang into action. We walked out of the house five minutes later, and we got to Austin in under two hours. We wanted to meet the doctor and be there for Avery's surgery. On the way we called my mom, who went over to our house to take care of things there.

Avery's jaw was wired shut for eight weeks—what a nightmare. Thanksgiving rolled around during this time, and I remember putting turkey, mashed potatoes, and cranberries in the blender, and he drank it through a straw. Disgusting ... but what other option did he have if he wanted to participate in the Thanksgiving feast?

What I learned from this experience is that there is this nifty little feature on our cell phones called "Favorites." When this feature is turned on, anyone you designate as a favorite will be allowed to ring through, even if your phone is silenced. I seriously wish I'd known about this sooner.

You'd think this incident would have warned them off of college-game behavior, but no, the games continued. One night at a party where college-age testosterone was raging, an alcohol-fueled conversation began about a punching bag that was hanging at a downtown bar in Austin. One thing led to another, and a competition began over how hard each guy could hit the bag. When it was Ryan's turn, he approached the bag, wound up, and blasted it as hard as he could— except he missed the bag and hit the side of the machine. Thankfully this time the Favorites feature woke us when he called in the middle of the night.

When we got to the hospital, we learned that he had fractured his wrist, which again brought with it a complicated healing process. I intentionally did not make things easy for him. One of my favorite quotes is "If you're going to be stupid, you better be tough," and I wanted him to see that there were consequences to stupid behavior. We got him an orthopedic surgeon in Houston, five minutes from our home, and he had to drive in from Austin every Friday to see the doctor and get X-rays—when he didn't have class and could be enjoying some free time—ha! It was nine months of headache, and we were glad when it was finally over.

It didn't take long for Ryan, officially my try-any-outdoor-sport kid, to end up back in the ER. He had gotten a new longboard, and he was obsessed with riding. He was practicing well into the night, and his practice spot was near the UT campus in Austin. If you know anything about the streets of Austin, there are a lot of potholes, and in the dark he couldn't see them. While he was cruising along, one wheel lodged into one of these potholes, and the longboard came to a jarring stop. Ryan was thrown, and his shoulder crashed into the cement curb, breaking his collarbone. We spent more time driving to Austin to manage injuries during the college years than anything else!

Tip: once they turn eighteen, the doctor will no longer give you any information about their health, due to HIPAA. At this stage they must be able to manage their own doctor visits, which can come as a shock to both them and you. Not a bad idea to get a power of attorney for healthcare to allow you to help them legally.

STAYING CLOSE IN THE COLLEGE YEARS

When young men and women reach the college years, and most definitely in young adulthood, their schedules take on a life of their own: school, work, relationships, self-care, hobbies, etc. Again, this can be disconcerting. We want them to grow up, and part of adulthood is a busy life—nevertheless it hurts when their schedules no longer revolve around ours.

We decided early on that we wanted to remain close throughout these years, so we came up with a few strategies to help establish this practice.

CHOOSE A NIGHT FOR FAMILY FACETIME CALLS

To combat this in the college years, choose one night every week for family FaceTime calls. If you do this with your first child, it trains the others automatically that this is what's expected when they go off to college. The beauty of this practice is it becomes a habit. For instance, when Avery was in college, we made this FaceTime appointment with him every Sunday night. When Ryan went to college, he just automatically did the same thing.

Each Sunday we had family FaceTime from wherever they were. The rest of the family would sit down to dinner, place the phone on a lazy Susan, then spin it around, so we could all say hi. Avery is now twenty-five years old and lives on the other side of the country. He has a great job; he's in a steady relationship; and he has a full life. Yet every Sunday at about dinnertime, he still calls home. That's the beauty of scheduling a set time every week for these calls.

FAMILY TEXTS

Each family member, of course, texts each other individually, and the texts between the brothers seem to be very special. What we discovered as a way to keep the whole family close, as a unit, was the family group text. We find it keeps us connected on daily issues. I might let them know about a new niece or a spectacular sunset Scott and I are witnessing. They might text about some fun plans they have over the weekend or a memory from childhood that comes out of nowhere (those are the best). The other day, in fact, Avery was at a concert, and he texted us some amazing pics from the event.

I feel strongly about my tip for this section: the text is great, and it can easily keep everyone up to date on general issues. The text, however, cannot and should not replace the voice-to-voice phone call. I play devil's advocate all the time on this because I believe one of my roles as a mom is to keep my children close.

> **The text cannot and should not replace the voice-to-voice phone call.**

I might casually suggest, "Reece, when was the last time you talked to your brother in Austin?" If he's been speaking to him regularly, great, but more often than not, they need a little nudge: "It wouldn't be a bad idea to call him, see how the new apartment is." I may hear some hemming and hawing, but then, later on, I'll hear them laughing and talking on the phone. Mission accomplished!

COLLEGE VISITS FROM THE FAMILY

Visiting your kids in college is another way to bond and make lasting memories. It's the first time, in most cases, that they get to show you their world. Make the time special for them, and be sure to encourage them regarding any positive lifestyle choices.

What we found to be a doubly effective strategy was having the brothers visit their older siblings at college. When Reece visited Avery in Nashville, it was truly touching to see how they bonded. If you recall, Reece is my celiac, and Avery had gluten-free restaurants already lined up to take care of his brother.

Besides this bonding (which will always be the priority in our moms' hearts), there is a practical result to allowing younger siblings to visit older siblings in college: they get to experience some of what to expect when they reach college.

My tip: encourage your precollege high schooler to visit with older college siblings or responsible friends. Let them experience the size and feel of a college campus, which is often overwhelming. Give them the experience of cheering on the football team and going to college events. We found that this slow initiation was the best way to prepare them for the newness of college and get them excited about the experience.

STAYING CLOSE IN THE YOUNG ADULT STAGE

Credit for this strategy goes to a wonderful couple, Lynelle and Kelly, who we've been friends with for years. It just so happens that their kids are about five years older than ours, so they were able to provide some tips for what's to come.

As your college-age children begin graduating and starting their own lives for real, you may need to get a bit tricky in order to keep them close. Relationships and friend groups take up their limited spare time, and you likely want to stay relevant. The trick is to lure them in by having—or obtaining—"the place to be." Let me explain this:

THE "PLACE TO BE": OBTAIN IT WITH VACATIONS/HOLIDAY GETAWAYS

Shamelessly lure them to you with vacations to exciting new places or familiar old ones. For instance, my kids love Costa Rica. So maybe I would say, "We're going to Costa Rica; do y'all want to go? We'll rent a big house on the beach and do some waterskiing and boating." All of a sudden, the "need to spend time with family" becomes the highlight of the season. The conversations and sharing of the excitement may last all year as the trip is planned and discussions about possible future destinations ensue.

The same thing can be done during the holidays. Scott's parents did this for us, and the good times and memories are priceless, especially now that my mother-in-law's health prohibits her from traveling any longer. Every December at around the same time, they took us on a cruise. We snorkeled, ziplined, and enjoyed those wonderful buffets together. When they suggested this as a yearly holiday gift, we jumped at it. Like fishermen with a hook, they lured us right in.

My tip here is that this type of experience can be accomplished without overwhelming your budget on expensive vacations. Try renting a cabin for a weekend at your local campgrounds; maybe you can have a great dinner at a sought-after restaurant; or cook up their favorite foods and lure them with a day of "football and favorite foods." For example, my mother makes the most amazing empanadas, and when she's got them on her menu, it always brings our boys together.

It doesn't really matter how much money you spend making family time special; the trick is to provide the events that lure them your way.

THE "PLACE TO BE": OWN IT!

Along the same lines, owning "the party place," say the condo on the beach or the cabin in the mountains, will lure your kids and their families to you on a regular basis. We're not talking about having them throw wild parties with friends; we're talking about a place with great attractions that the family looks forward to getting together at. I'm told that once the grandchildren come, this type of situation is ideal for everyone, as it's actually more cost-effective in the end.

My tip: be sure your schedule coincides with theirs! Remember that they have jobs, possibly families at this point, and full lives of their own. You may also still be working and have a full schedule. Be sure you have the same availability that they do to get the most out of sharing your time at your family party place.

KEEP IT *ONE*, BIG, HAPPY FAMILY

When Scott and I got married, we blended families, meaning his parents and siblings have become close to mine. We foster this atmosphere by simply including everyone in both families in our events and holidays. We celebrate both Christian and Jewish holidays, so my mom has everyone out for Rosh Hashanah and Christmas; my sister-in-law takes on the same crowd at Thanksgiving; Scott's cousin hosts Passover celebration in April; then back to my mom for Easter; and I have everyone for Yom Kippur and Hanukkah. We're talking my whole side, plus Scott's, which means Scott's parents, uncles, aunts, and cousins. Everyone brings their specialty dish, and I look forward to them all! In this way our family stays close, and I hope to enlarge our family even more by inviting my daughters-in-law to be a part of it.

I'm told that, in general, young men who find "the one" gravitate toward her family and their traditions. I want to have a part in that too! I plan to unite the families as best I can by inviting them to our celebrations.

Tip #1: obviously, including extended family in your celebrations can mean a lot of people gathering. If your home isn't equipped to handle such a crowd, consider renting a room in a restaurant or hall.

Tip #2: in order to be sure not to interfere with other already-established holiday plans, consider choosing a different calendar day for your event than the actual day when everyone else is celebrating.

WHEN THEY FINALLY GET IT!

Once your young adult reaches their midtwenties, they begin to understand and appreciate all you did to raise them to a safe, stable place in adulthood. There certainly were times when Scott and I questioned if this would ever be the case.

Just at the age of twenty-two, when Avery was out of college, it seemed like a light bulb went on, and he wrote Scott a card, explaining how much Scott's influence meant to him. It was so beautiful, I framed it and hung it right by Scott's bathroom sink, so he can see it every time he washes his hands.

Avery obviously learned from what he saw Scott doing and is now doing it with his younger brothers. He wished he'd had an older sibling give him some words of wisdom before he went off to college. So, with Reece just starting his freshman year, Avery thought to send him this text:

Hey Kid, hope you're settling into college well. I never had an older brother to pass down advice to me, so I wanted to pass along some wisdom. Obviously, UT and Vandy are very different schools, but I think the following pieces of advice are helpful no matter what. Feel free to copy this into your phone notes if you want to look back on these.

LEARN HOW TO TEACH YOURSELF THE MATERIAL: Professors aren't always the best teachers. And very easy to zone out in larger lectures. Don't expect to come away from classes knowing material. You'll have to stay on top of the reading yourself unfortunately. If you feel super behind before the midterm, just block out a day to catch up on everything.

WORK SMARTER, NOT HARDER: Find a study buddy, preferably smarter than you, preferably not even someone you hang out with socially. Get their notes/study guide. Online quizlets. Go to office hours, and buddy up with TA/professor if you can.

DECIPHER BETWEEN INTENTIONAL SOCIAL ACTIVITIES VS. POINTLESS SOCIAL ACTIVITIES: Freshman year, there is a lot of free booling going on. Late nights just hanging with buddies and playing video games. Definitely enjoy some of that when you're meeting people this fall, but also know your boys will be your boys. Get boiling good grades your freshman year because 1) they are prob the easiest classes you will take and 2) as you become an upperclassman, your schedule will be filled with "intentional" social activities (mixers, date parties, frat events). You don't want to have to miss these because you missed the mark freshman year on grades.

DON'T BE THAT GUY: In risky, late-night situations with alcohol. Scootering, driving, fights, breaking into places. It's okay to be mixed up in that sometimes, but don't be THAT GUY. AKA, don't be bold in risky situations for a laugh or because you were ignorant to the situation.

BE THE GUY: Nice and friendly to everyone. BE the friend. TO EVERYONE. Everyone has something to offer you.

ONE CLUB: Doesn't have to be freshman year, but try to get involved in one org outside of ZBT or Mccombs. Where you can meet different sets of people.

- If you hate everyone, eat a meal.
- If you think everyone hates you, go to sleep.
- If you hate yourself, take a shower.

This is the same son whose middle school attitude single-handedly wrecked a trip to Costa Rica, the same one who angrily criticized, "Why couldn't y'all just be real parents and tell me I needed to go to UT?"

They do come to a point where they get it! This past Valentine's Day, Avery surprised me by mailing me a beautiful Valentine Le Fleur, which is a rose that retains its fragrance for a year. I never even made a fuss over Valentine's Day when they were kids. It was completely unexpected and something I cherish. And for my birthday, Ryan mailed me flowers and Reece surprised me with a Happy box.

They really do come to appreciate you! All the training, counseling, and consistency that made everyone crazy become worth it when it comes full circle, and your young adult is on the right path for their life.

• • •

JOURNALING IN THE COLLEGE AND YOUNG ADULT STAGE

PROOF IT WORKS!

You might recall that at one point I had all our home movies put on USB drives in chronological order. Out of the blue, Avery asked me about those USBs. He was interested in having his copy—remember, at twenty-five, he gets it.

I resisted at first, cautioning him about how precious they were. I'm so glad I entrusted it to him. I thought he'd put it in his desk somewhere and forget about it. Instead about a month later, he started texting us clips of, say, a family vacation with a message like, "Remember when Ryan got that splinter in his foot?"

They often go back and watch these videos for hours, sharing different memories. We're all crying and laughing together at our respective ends, and it's exactly what I wanted and why I went to such lengths to keep up my journal. Proof like this shows me it works!

CONCLUSION

It has truly been my pleasure to spend time sharing with you about motherhood through the years. I hope you leave these pages with an arsenal of tips for you to reach for during your motherhood journey. As I close the book and think about what those journeys might look like, I want to encourage you that every sacrifice you make as a parent is a step forward for your child—even if they don't always recognize that. Sometimes it seems children are literally designed to make us, as parents, stretch.

I recall Ryan having a very different mindset than we did, and it was a constant battle to rein in some wilder tendencies. At one point in college, he informed us that he now knew why this tension existed between us. He had taken the "Myers-Briggs Type Indicator," a personality-assessment test, and determined that he was literally created different. I believe his phrasing went something like, "You're a Type-A, and I'm a Type-Z. The only thing I can say about that is don't be a Karen."

So if I asked the waitress for the gluten-free menu, he was right away accusing me of being a Karen. It took me several internet searches to understand what he meant. Then I assessed it. A "Karen" is a demanding bitch who considers no one but herself. I admit I do speak up for my kids. I do make mention if something can hurt them—and I don't really care who likes it or doesn't. If that makes us "Kevin and Karen," I'm okay with that, and I'll keep doing it without giving in to any shame.

BAD-PARENT MOMENTS

Speaking of giving in to the shame on your parenting journey, there will likely be a few moments you aren't so proud of. These moments happen to us all, and they're rarely intended, but oh, the guilt they can create!

When Ryan was an infant, we gated Avery in his room to avoid him going into the nursery to "play" unsupervised with his new baby brother. He stood at the gate screaming night after night, and we assessed the behavior to be tantrums over the gate. We firmly told him to go back to bed; we were in charge; he wasn't leaving his room right now—typically an effective parenting technique—except when they are sick and trying to tell you about it.

A few days later, we came to discover that a raging ear infection had been developing. Here we were concentrating on discipline, and he needed antibiotics. We were beside ourselves with guilt—so much so that Scott came home that night with a six-foot, gray-and-white, shaggy stuffed dog from FAO Schwarz. We couldn't tell him enough how sorry we were.

How about when Ryan was nine months old? I was putting Avery to bed, so Scott took Ryan out of the room. All of a sudden, I heard this scream from Ryan. He never cried, so I went running. There was Scott, holding him, visibly feeling horrible.

Ryan had been holding a drumstick, and it jammed him in the throat as dad placed him on the floor. We looked in his mouth, and my finger scooped out a lot of blood. A lot of screaming and hyperventilating ensued, but thankfully the baby was okay ... Scott, however, has never been the same.

You'd think by this time, four sons later and writing a book on parenting, I'd be past mistakes, cruising down the motherhood highway, unfettered and error-free. Not so much. Just last week I was out to dinner with Ryan and jumped to a few unfair conclusions regarding his personal life. It was one of those moments when the look on his face legitimately told me I got it wrong this time. I had to apologize to him right then and there.

Forgive yourself, apologize if you have to, and always move forward.

Parents, you will mess up—that's a fact. Life didn't come with a manual; it came with a mom—and she's imperfect and human, but she loves her kids like no one else in the world ever will. My tip: forgive yourself, apologize if you have to, and always move forward.

TAKE FIVE

My last tip for the book is to learn, as a mom, to step back for a moment and take five when you feel your temper flaring—and I'm not only talking about losing it with your kids. Other parents can cause the mama bear to take over your being and roar. I recall being at the park when someone got in one of my sons' faces about getting dirt on her daughter's princess dress. First of all it's a playground; I'm not saying don't wear the dress, but you better know it's going to get dirty. I marched right over and told her, pretty fiercely, to speak to me if she has a problem with my child's actions; I'll discipline my own child, if needed.

These types of incidents happened more frequently than I was comfortable admitting, and Scott noticed it too. It's just that these are my kids, and any criticism or perceived threat to them caused a wall of defense to rise up. Any other moms out there know exactly what I'm talking about? I know you do.

On the flipside, of course, are these very children, who you'd fight someone else to protect, that can cause the same quick temper. A million scenarios can cause you to lose your cool, and if you have hot blood like I do, it's something to get control of. But how?

There is magic in taking five minutes—or sometimes just five seconds because that's all you've got—to remove yourself from the situation and get a hold of that temper. Oftentimes you will see that things aren't such a big deal after all. Better yet you may come up with a really good creative response to whatever irked you once your rational brain takes over.

FINAL THOUGHTS: CONSISTENCY REALLY DOES PAY OFF!

During Ryan's first week as a freshman at UT, he became somewhat of a mentor to his three roommates. Why? Was it excellence in his studies or on the sports field? No … it was something much more basic: his dorm room came equipped with a washer and dryer. No problem at all for him—but none of his three roommates knew how to wash clothes! One day he FaceTimed me as a college freshman and said he was teaching his roomies how to wash. He found himself creating tutorials on the whole process. He was pretty proud of himself, and so were we. All those summers of telling him to sort and wash and monitor the dryer, and it did in fact pay off! (Come to think of it, I also made a Laundry 101 sheet, and Reece took it to college and taped it to his washer door.)

When it's all said and done, repetition and consistency will produce the best results in parenting. All the training, from sleeping during infancy to chores to requiring a family night, are steps you build on to make your life easier. The open communication, safe house, and directly facing even the squeamish subjects are to maintain a good relationship with your kids, because once they walk out that door, life's choices will hit them relentlessly. As moms we hope and pray that they hear our guiding voice when those decisions face them, that they rely on the values we instilled in them, and that they gained the necessary wisdom from our mothering year by year.

Dawson (15), Reece (18), Scott, Jenn, Ryan (22), and Avery (24).

THE END

TIRAS FAMILY QUOTES

If you're gonna be stupid, you better be tough.

No one has ever drowned in their own sweat.

We learn a lot more from our failures than we do our successes.

If people perceive you are successful,
you will indeed become successful.

Bite off more than you can chew and then chew like hell.

The expert in anything was once a beginner.

A smile is an inexpensive way to improve your looks.

People want to do stuff for people they like, be likeable.

You will never get in trouble for something you didn't say.

Failure isn't failure if a lesson from it is learned.

There is no such thing as 99 percent integrity.

People do stuff for people they like.

What happened today in the present that seems so terrible
will soon become the past.

That which does not kill you makes you stronger.

At the end of the day, your favorite sport better be math.

If you get it wrong, just get it right next time.

You learn by listening.

All the things you did when nobody was watching
will help you when everybody's watching.

Be careful what you tell anybody, as they will tell everybody.

Spend less money than you make and save the difference.

If you work two extra hours a day than they guy next door,
you should do better as it adds up to three extra months'
worth of work per year.

You have to place the order if you are going to get served.

You will not get everything you want
but it doesn't mean you can't try to.

Perception is 95 percent truth.

If you want something done, give it to a busy person.

The only thing I know for sure is that I don't know anything for sure.

When you have little kids they have little problems;
when they are bigger kids, they have bigger problems.

You are only as happy as your unhappiest child.

Everyone is attracted to a great BIG smile.

You can never let your talent take you someplace
that your character can't keep you.

The only good loser IS a loser.

Do not corner something that you know is meaner than you.

As you walk by someone in the hallway,
make eye contact and say hello with a smile.

Don't tell people your problems, as 20 percent of them don't care
and the other 80 percent are glad you have them.

I will give you every tool you need to build your own house
but you have to do the building.

Don't ask why but when you turn 50, you become invisible.

Take deep breaths often, count to ten. You will feel better.

There are very few people that want you to succeed, understand
that most want you to fail even when they say otherwise.

Don't give a dog a biscuit for pissing in the kitchen.

When taking your car in (or getting something fixed),
it's not whether you are getting screwed, it's just how bad.

People like being around happy people, fake it.

School is not about learning the material it's about learning
"HOW TO" learn the material.

As bad as something seems, time will fix it.

Be a man of your word, have integrity and character in all you do.

When starting out, you will only be successful in an organization if you make your superiors look good.

There are two types of successful people:
(1) either you are so good and smart that others need your input (Jobs) or (2) you better be "good enough," work hard, add value and be able to deal with others.

Everyone thinks their job is important, make them think you agree even if you don't.

Never respond to irritating email or text immediately, give it at least 30 minutes.

Never put anything in writing that you don't want shared.

Loose lips sink ships (be careful what you tell other people as it can backfire).

With very few exceptions, always return emails, texts and phone calls, especially the ones you don't want to.

When making any commitment (even one you don't think is important), do what you say when you say you will and in a timely manner (absent a family emergency).

If you wrong someone, personally meet with them, look them in the eye and apologize.

Misery loves company.

Nobody who ever gave his best regretted it.

Build up your weaknesses until they become your strong points.

There are 86,400 seconds in a day.
It's up to you to decide what to do with them.

He who takes on the most sh-t deserves to get paid the most.

Some of Gods greatest gifts are unanswered prayers.

Every time the market has gone down, it's gone back up
and at some point will hit a new high again.

Just remember that everyone is out to F....you (kind of).

You are responsible for your reputation.
Once you do something, you can never "unring that bell".

Sometimes when you are feeling down (and yes this will happen
some), it's good to take a step back and think about all you HAVE
accomplished instead of what you haven't.

Never do ANYTHING you don't want read about on the front page
of the Wall Street Journal or see on the 10 o'clock news.

You are measured by the company you keep.

Email is a bad way to communicate or discuss a delicate
or difficult problem. Deal with problems in person or over the phone.

Nothing good happens after midnight.

You may not be able to fish or fix a tire so you better be able to add
and subtract like a M..F....

There are no coincidences.

The only person you are destined to become
is the person you decide to be.

Everything always works out for the best.

No good deed goes unpunished.

Dance with the one that brung ya.

If someone offers you something and it seems
too good to be true, it usually is!

Say your prayers daily.

Sometimes what seems SO important today
(I mean life changing), really is not that important tomorrow.

You don't always get a trophy.

Don't take rejection personally,
it's just part of life and knocks out the weak.

You have to market yourself as you are responsible
for your own success.

Attitude is everything, have a good attitude.

You're never in too big of a hurry in a car to where you might
run over some kid playing in the street, change your life
and theirs forever. Don't speed, you'll get there.

Life feels like a contact sport sometimes.

When dating, it's ok the throw a few lines out there
and see what's biting.

Your mouth can get you into more trouble than just about
anything else you can do so quit telling people stuff.

It's ok to step out of your comfort zone and test yourself.
Sometimes the ball goes between your legs and sometimes
you hit a home run but how you ever gonna know if you don't try.

Over prepare (for a test or presentation), you'll be glad you did.

Everyone wants to live on top of the mountain, but all the happiness
and growth occurs while you're climbing it.

It's not that I thought I could do it, just never thought I couldn't.

Other people have had your problems before and
managed to overcome them. You can too.

In order to have good things, there must be bad things.

Anything you post or type via the internet "THEY" can find
(even if you think it's deleted, it's not).

There is no elevator to success you must take steps,
sometimes a bunch of them, actually!

I am happy I have a relatively simple life and am
willing to work hard! The easy path leads to the hard life,
the hard path leads to the easy life.

Practice like someone is always watching you.

Always loo k way ahead, as the future soon becomes the present
(plan ahead as time creeps up quickly).

It's not the will to win that matters, everyone has that.
It's the "will to prepare" to win that matters.

Do what is right even when no one is looking.

Today is going to suck A LOT, that's why they made tomorrow!

If someone wanted to talk to you tomorrow,
they would have called, texted or emailed you tomorrow.
But since they reached out to you today, they probably want to talk
to you today. Respond to them today!

In everything you do, have a PLAN B.

If you have to borrow for it, don't buy it.

Ask people a lot of questions about themselves.
People will like you when you let them talk about themselves.

When you are young you compete with your physical strength,
when you get older you compete with your mental strength.
Work on building your mental muscle now,
you will be glad you did.

Become an EXPERT in something (get in your 10,000 hours).

There are not too many things that can make a good life bad
but a few are... getting addicted to drugs, driving under the
influence, or an unwanted pregnancy. These are bells that
are hard to get unrung.

Never underestimate the power of an apology.

Be the first person to say hello in an elevator.

Whatever you are as y ou become older you become more of.

Don't settle for average, as there is so much more.

You don't have to like me, you just have to listen to me
(tell your kids).

If you keep doing what you have always done, you will keep getting what you have always gotten (maybe change something if you don't like where you are at).

You get more with sugar than you do with vinegar.

When managing someone, give them five parts sugar with every piece of vinegar (tell them five good things for every bad).

Life is all about experiences, go get some experiences and embrace them (yes even the bad ones).

One of the most important things that you can do in life is being needed and necessary (have a challenging job and good family).

You can't experience success until you have first experienced failure.

You cannot unsay a cruel word.

Live a good, honorable life... Then when you get older and think back, you'll enjoy it a second time.

Lettin' the cat outta the bag is a whole lot easier than puttin' it back in.

The difference between a successful person and others is not a lack of strength, not a lack of knowledge but a lack of will.

What happened yesterday is history.
What happens tomorrow is a mystery.
What we do today makes the difference.

Make each day your masterpiece.

Don't be in awe of anyone. Nobody is that special.

Future pain is inevitable at some point in your life,
suffering is optional.

Friends inspire you or they drain you, pick them wisely.

Early in career it's important to fit life into your work and not
work into your life (work hard).

Be kind as everyone you meet/know is fighting a very fierce battle.

Be There for other people, show up, be on time
and be that shoulder for them.

Early in your career be the first person at work
and one of the last to le ave. It will be noticed.

It's easy to see the bright side of other people's problems.

How you ever gonna know if you never dare to try.

The hard path leads to the easy life and the easy path to the hard.

Those who forget the past are condemned to repeat it.

You have to ask yourself, do you want to spend the rest of your life
signing the front of the check or the back?

There's never just one cockroach in the kitchen.

Train people well enough so they can leave.
Treat them well enough so they don't want to.

In a negotiation, never make the first offer.

When entrusted with a secret, keep it.

You marry the girl, you marry her whole family.

If you're the smartest person in the room, you're in the wrong room.

You're entitled to nothing; be grateful for everything.

Read CNN and CNBC for twenty minutes every day
so you can talk about most anything with clients/friends
(ESPN for 10 can't hurt).

Every strike gets you that much closer to hitting the home run.

Just know that your shyness looks a lot like arrogance
to someone else.

Take a chance and go out on a limb as that is where all the fruit is.

The difference between a successful person and others is
not a lack of strength, not a lack of knowledge but rather
a lack of will.

Nobody who ever gave his best ever regretted it.

Once you learn to quit, it becomes a habit.

Failures are expected by loser and ignored by winners.

Life is not tried, it is merely survived, if you are
standing outside the fire.

You can't go back and change the beginning so start now
so you can change the ending.

How old would you be if you didn't know the day you were born!

Having someone in your life not to disappoint, makes you better.

Anything that can't last forever, Won't.

You cannot make a good deal with a bad person.

Dress for the job that you want, not the one you have.

If you can't beat the fear then just do it scared.

Where you are today (good or bad)
is the result of all your prior decisions.

Stay away from negative people,
as they have a problem for every solution.

Experience is the hardest kind of teacher.
It gives you the text and the lesson afterwards.